DISCOVERING SHAKESPEARE

Discovering Shakespeare

A New Guide to the Plays

JOHN RUSSELL BROWN

M

© John Russell Brown 1981

First published 1981 by
THE MACMILLAN PRESS LTD
London and Basingstoke
Companies and representatives throughout the world

ISBN 0 333 31633 9 (hc)
ISBN 0 333 31634 7 (pbk)

Printed and bound in Great Britain
at The Pitman Press, Bath

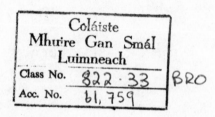

Contents

Preface

Readers who are familiar with professional scholarship and criticism will appreciate how much I have benefited in writing this book from the work of others who have studied Shakespeare's plays in performance. Other readers who work in theatre will recognise just as easily how much I owe to the actors, directors, designers and stage-staff with whom I have worked on productions and in workshops. I hope, too, that my students and colleagues at the University of Sussex and at the Folger Library, Washington D.C. will realise that I have shared my thoughts and methods of study with them, and gained by the exchange.

Indeed, in preparing this book, I have drawn on such a wide experience that I am quite unable to trace the beginning or development of each idea or start to acknowledge my innumerable debts. I cannot express adequately a gratitude of which I am constantly aware. By great good fortune, this new guide to Shakespeare's plays is a product of a long collaboration. It is wholly mine only in the writing.

Two particular debts I can, however, acknowledge and do so with grateful pleasure: to Penny Admiraal for typing out my first drafts and corrections; and to Derick Mirfin of Macmillan for guiding the book from typescript to its final form with uncommon vigilance and generosity.

JOHN RUSSELL BROWN

NOTE ON TEXTS

References to Shakespeare's texts in this book are to *The Complete Works* edited by Peter Alexander (Collins, London and Glasgow, 1951), save for those instances, clearly indicated, where a different edition is cited for particular comment.

1 | *Introduction*

Our response to Shakespeare's plays has been changing slowly, and with difficulty, during the last twenty years, but now the time has come for a decisive revolution.

Readers and critics have become increasingly aware that the plays were written for performance and reveal their true natures only in performance. We have adapted our study accordingly, modifying literary criticism as best we can and remembering, whenever possible, to pay attention to stage-directions, meaningful gestures, impressive silences, and other theatrical features. But that, I believe, is no longer good enough. I have based this new guide on a new premise: that we should read and study the plays as if we were rehearsing them, and that we should then attempt to imagine performances. I have tried to show how every reader can use imagination and experience in the same way as an actor does, and how everyone can learn from what happens in a theatre during performance. So the texts of Shakespeare's plays can reveal living images of life.

Occasionally I take issue with other books and with current methods of editing or criticism, but I have no wish to denigrate Shakespearean scholarship and literary expertise. If this new road to a fuller enjoyment is followed, many earlier studies will contribute in new ways to the different engagement.

Part of the revolution I seek is a change of priorities. Character-analysis and the search for an underlying theme must wait until after the play has begun to come alive in a reader's imagination – with all the excitement and strength of theatrical performance, and with the sudden revelations and slow revaluations which are the ordinary signs of vitality in rehearsal. Semantic footnotes must be relegated to a position consonant with a primary concern for speech and action; they must not be allowed to shoulder out of sight the textual difficulties that are discovered in rehearsal. A reader's enquiry about a text is not finished when all the hard words are made plain; this should be a continous accompaniment to the more extraordinary and more demanding task of exploring the many ways in which an actor can breathe life into the words, the many indications in the text of how an actor should speak his lines, and the many clues to what should happen on stage. As hard words are only a small part of speech, so speech is only part of continual stage-action; and individual actors are only a part of the interactions of a number of actors who are each informed by the words of the complete text and each full of independent, creative energies.

The basis of this new guide to Shakespeare's plays is the art of the actor. By adapting an actor's means of exploration to his own needs, a reader can 'possess' a text in a lively and personal way, and start upon his own act of discovery. But a reader must also respond like an audience and develop, as a modern director will do, a sense of the whole: the interaction of performances, the effect of spectacle, rhythm and music, the varying focus and the changes in an audience's sense of illusion and reality, lies and truth.

Occasionally I propose very painstaking work, which many readers of this book will lack time to undertake, but I do not wish to undervalue a simple reading of a text which accepts whatever pleasures occur naturally and easily; indeed I argue that this should be a repeated element of any serious exploration. I hope that my readers will be led to a reappraisal of Shakespeare's plays by the argument of the whole book and by the new readings of some of the greatest of them with which it is illustrated; I also hope that they will be drawn into the more difficult ways of study that I propose, by making discoveries for themselves wherever this guide speaks most usefully to them. I trust they will then find their own, less methodical, ways of responding to the texts.

It is commonly said that the pleasure of reading Shakespeare and the rarer pleasure of seeing a wonderful production of one of his plays are distinct from one another. Frequently the gap is huge, but the two experiences should be of the same kind and draw strength from each other. Performance is set over against reading only because the texts are often read and studied as if they were long poems or most peculiar novels. This book tries to give a theatrical understanding to readers and to introduce ways of developing a theatrical imagination in order that readers and playgoers alike may enjoy the plays as mirrors that reflect, in animated and revealing detail, the world we live in and ourselves.

2 | *Shakespeare Dead and Alive*

Shakespeare's texts are alive on the stage, as part of living images of life itself. New revelations are registered with each theatrical season as actors, designers, directors, musicians and managers collaborate in the endless quest for productions that will engage their audiences. But, in our minds, as we respond to performances, there is a still more various and intimate life. All theatrical realities and limitations may be forgotten, as the plays are recreated in our imaginations, drawing on whatever we have experienced or dreamed before that time of performance. An exhilarating interplay between these elements – Shakespeare's text, its theatrical enactment and our own thoughts and feelings – can transport us into a fabulous world, full of surprises and deep pleasures. This book is about that process.

Staging the plays is the surest means of bringing them to life, but it is neither the only one nor the most generally available. Millions who have never entered a theatre appreciate Shakespeare's writings. Millions of playgoers enjoy the experience of reading the texts when they are at home or alone. In these private encounters we progress at our own pace, wherever and whenever we please. Personal involvement can then be strongest – unless we are among the few who perform on stage – and the plays are then most capable of reflecting our own concerns, transforming, enriching and clarifying them. I think, too, that an imaginative response to reading the plays is the most likely way to catch an impresssion of the very sound, the unique touch, of Shakespeare's own voice. This may be true even for actors, because the practicalities of stage-craft and the limits of personal achievement do not intrude at those times, or deflect attention. Certainly the plays can be vitally alive as we read with performance in mind, and this book is about that process too. I want to consider how best to read, what kinds of attention are good, what specialised knowledge is helpful, and the reasons for all this.

I will also argue that there are times when we should examine the plays as if they were inert, a sequence of words or arrangements of letters

3

on the page of a book, all of equal size and style, static, definite and open
to prolonged enquiry. Such an objective scrutiny is not so easy as it may
sound, because the dead text of Shakespeare's plays is very unlike an
ordinary corpse. It has an obstinate way of returning to life as a play in
our minds, even as we study it meticulously, counting its commas or
noting its auxiliary verbs. But the distinction between death and life
should be remembered, because only when we observe the plays as fixed
objects can we be precise and definite, or pay attention to problems
involving the transmission of what Shakespeare actually wrote, the
errors of scribes and compositors, the relevance and varying authority of
stage-directions and punctuation, the possible suggestions or impreci-
sions of each word free from the constraints and influences of its
dramatic context. Much of this study is highly specialist and takes more
time than most of us can spare, but every reader can enjoy some
dissection. These enquiries have their own fascination, as myriads of
linguistic possibilities are revealed and the sharp, minutely crafted
substance of the text is more precisely appreciated. The words
themselves can hold our attention, on their own account, without the
constantly changing and finally elusive images which are the concomm-
itant life they were designed to have in our minds. This book is also
about these investigations, when for short periods we actually possess
and master the words that Shakespeare wrote and they stop dead in
their tracks.

The fact that the corpse won't lie down, that the distinction between
Shakespeare dead and alive has to be carefully watched and protected,
signals one of the first assumptions to be made in our approach to the
plays. When a scholar wants to trace the progress of a broken piece of
type used in the original printing and is peering into a composite
photographic image of multiple copies of a first edition, a light may
flash suddenly in his mind rather than on the screen. This reader is not
trying to wrest a meaning from the text and is careless of his imaginative
engagement, but some phrase springs into unquestionable life, awaken-
ing earlier memories or striking new conceptions in some unforeseen and
challenging way. Such unscheduled moments of creative response are
often deep because they are uncensored, and they can make a lasting
impression. What is true for the bibliographer can also be true for any
other reader. Anyone who enjoys the plays in the theatre where they are
most alive will profit by spending some time in more objective, more
'deadly' pursuits.

Certainly we must not always try to wrest a meaning out of
Shakespeare's plays or strive to possess them thoroughly. We should

allow them to surprise us by remaining open to unexpected suggestion. Near the beginning of his career, Shakespeare gave Berowne in *Love's Labour's Lost* a warning against laborious study:

> Small have continual plodders ever won,
> Save base authority from others' books,   ... (I i 86–7)

(According to the *Oxford English Dictionary*, the word 'plodder' first entered the language in that sentence.)

A new guide to Shakespeare's plays must start by emphasising the need to remain open to whatever the plays offer, however strange that may seem. We should be watchful when we stumble on hitherto unnoticed words and phrases, or on the necessity of silence; or when we catch strange echoes between scene and scene, or find ourselves misreading a speech or entertaining apparently unconnected ideas and images. In one of his last plays, *Cymbeline*, Shakespeare has Pisanio make the outrageous claim that 'Fortune brings in some boats that are not steer'd' (IV iii 46), and goes on to prove him right by the action of the play. The same I think must be said of our attempts to understand and enjoy Shakespeare. We need good pilots and practice at the helm, but experience and strict study are by no means all-sufficient.

For example, we should value the general, confused impression of a first and perhaps hurried reading, as the unexplored territory of the text still lies stretched out before us. What we see then has the force and clarity of our first view of a country or city that we have never previously visited. Our minds seek a resting place but do not expect to feel at home; our senses are keyed up for adventure and responsive to new impressions.

I remember the first time I read *Much Ado About Nothing*. People were talking, lightly and continually; they were spirited and volatile, for ever moving in and out of sight. Sometimes a light would flash, but then this busy world became dark, crowded and heavily furnished. Occasionally I heard music, but it was quickly challenged by the pressures of words and actions as talkative people teased, taunted, questioned and attacked each other. Other passages were slow, heavy and sustained, very unlike the brittle instability of the rest of this play. And then, after a wordless dance, the play was over: something had happened off-stage that should not be considered until tomorrow, but somehow the other issues had been momentarily forgotten. The life of this comedy seemed fugitive, its brightest moments being the most unknowable, hidden behind many words, outbreaks of laughter, anger or triviality.

I first read *Julius Caesar* as a schoolboy; all my attention was on the role of Flavius which had been allotted to me when the class combined to read the play aloud. The first scene was difficult, almost unintelligible;

the next scene, when Flavius entered but said nothing, a let-down. The
rest has left no impression. When I next read the play, some ten years
later, the whole text seemed tough, long, tense and, somehow, white. I
hardly know, today, why it seemed so blanched, quiet and even eerie,
despite the large-scale and violent scenes. For all its broad scope, the
play made a narrow progress. Together with the obvious realignments
and manoeuvres of the main action, there was a series of small, hard,
vital centres of attention.

These first views must be criticised and often lost to sight, but they are
of crucial importance if the plays are to come alive in our own
individual imaginations. Even when we are familiar with a play and
return to read it again after two or three years, some sense of new
discovery will come immediately and we should try to retain it. On
reflection it may be very obvious: perhaps the way in which Othello is so
isolated in Acts IV and V, when many other characters are dropping
away. Or a re-reading may be dominated by the way in which Othello's
speech anchors progressively on grand and basic ideas: fool, devil, soul,
body, husband, wife, honest, good, life, death, heart, soul, heaven and
hell; towards the end splendid images still flare upwards – 'chaste stars',
'monumental alabaster', 'flaming minister', 'Promethean heat' – but
the key words are devastatingly simple: cause, soul, blood, die, light,
love, weep. Recognition of these basic facts may spark off a new set of
questions: how many Othellos have spent their tears as fast their final
words indicate? How many have moved in their last moments with the
huge weight and delicacy – the fine judgement and intimacy – that
replace more raw and primitive passions? Sometimes a re-reading can
awaken an elementary question, not previously considered: for
example, 'Why should Othello die?'

Directors and actors, when beginning to work on one of
Shakespeare's plays, will cultivate consciously a fresh approach, and try
to read the text as if it were entirely new. This is not because they want
to be innovative or fashionable. They have to alert themselves just as
they are, just at that instant, to the task of staging the play: this will be,
inevitably, the grounds from which their production or performance
will spring. So should a student prize the effect of a 'first reading',
however much he changes this first view in the light of further analysis,
exploration, information, judgement, imagination and re-creation.

Shakespeare's plays should be alive in each individual mind. They
thrive in the level of our dreams and with the immediacy of our personal
and exact experience. A personal engagement must be sought from the
start, and renewed constantly.

☆

As time passes our view of each play will change, because we ourselves alter and our knowledge of the text becomes more complete. It will change, too, as we grow more capable of retaining more than a few plays in our minds at any one time. Whenever the life that we imagine in a play becomes fixed and familiar, it is time to question our engagement: we should probably turn to something else. Or we can read a scholarly book, or go to see a production.

Scholars often denounce theatre productions that give very slanted views of the plays: a cowboy *Much Ado*, a *Measure for Measure* set in the consulting rooms of Dr Freud's Vienna, an *As You Like It* as a baroque opera, or a *Hamlet* chopped up, weighted down with electronic theatricality, and served with a dash of obvious nudity, sadism or childish, bubbling vitality. Other Shakespeareans express their weariness with the long file of books, each one claiming to pluck the heart out of a complicated mystery. But these interpretative and explicatory excesses mark the essential diversity of the plays' appeal, and their tractability. If we hesitate before a transformation on stage or a narrow thesis in a well-argued book, it is the rider and not the horse that we should question and, if necessary, reject. Every new interpretation is calculated to catch our attention, and the best response is to welcome each as a new filter through which to see the plays for ourselves. When held between a viewer and an object, the filter obscures something and, at the same time, brings other features into unusual prominence. Tonal variations have been modified and so some features are obscured and something hitherto inconspicuous is lightened. We can enjoy any eccentric production or academic study, so long as we use it to quicken our own response. They all represent errors and perceptions other than our own, and so reveal aspects of the plays' life that we might never notice without their help or obstruction.

A natural desire in all students is to 'understand' a play and so possess it thoroughly. But this aim is possibly more foreign to the nature of Shakespeare's texts than the changing aspirations of the most individualistic theatre director. The study of Shakespeare is an endless quest which we must follow with enterprise and a kind of carelessness. Certainly it is a waste of time to fulminate against those who proclaim they have found the one secret or to barricade one's own temporary certainties against renewed attack. If statement is brought against statement, one filter replaced by another, a new look always encouraged, then direct engagement is more likely to follow and our pleasure to grow. Shakespeare should never be a closed subject in any mind.

So much is generally recognised in the busy theatrical profession. Only practical considerations of large auditoriums and the economics of play production prevent a revolution in our way of staging

Shakespeare. When a theatre director is producing a play for a long run in a modern theatre, certain ideas and discoveries have to be held firmly by everyone concerned; otherwise the expensive set will be found to be awkward, costumes and movements will express the wrong ideas, and the actors' confidence will be undermined. Naturally the plays are mettlesome in performance, changeable and enticing; always the author tends to be several steps ahead or to one side. Even when a director is restrained by practical considerations, his mind is liable to rush on ahead or retreat rashly from some expediency: certainties vanish from his mind.

John Barton, whose productions at Stratford-upon-Avon have seemed to be strong and clear, has protested vigorously that he is 'simply unable to form and articulate opinions about plays'. He was asked to lecture on the *Henry IV* plays, immediately after directing them; on being announced he stood up, but said nothing: 'I heard a little voice saying, I have no views on *Henry IV*. I paused for a long time, and said, "Any questions?".'[1]

Because of the nature of Shakespeare's mind and the theatrical medium for which he wrote, the aim of a student should be, not a settled understanding, but an imaginative and responsive engagement. Both reader and actor can enjoy a continuously changing and developing awareness of Shakespeare's text which draws on the individual's own experiences – literary, theatrical, political and personal – and interacts with them.

Shakespeare's writings are wide open to individual imaginative exploration. In part, this is a consequence of a life spent working for a theatre. Shakespeare knew how plays come alive on the stage and how actors create characters out of an interaction between the text and their own beings and imaginations. His theatre was different from any we know today, but the essential act of performance was the same. Plays were given an exact and personal life by the meeting of individual actors before particular audiences on specific days: they took on different appearances with each change in the cast and with each day of performance. The accident of an entry occurring a little earlier than usual could alter the effect (and therefore the meaning) of the following line. The comparative tiredness or vitality of the two actors in the last fight of *Hamlet* or *Macbeth* could swing an audience's sympathies in one direction or the other. An actor's hesitation could undermine the strength of an assertion or suggest a depth of feeling that could surprise the dramatist as much as an audience that was seeing the play for the first time. The mirror that a play holds up to human nature is not a scientific instrument but a part of nature itself, unpredictable and fascinating in its own being. A confident, accomplished dramatist will allow his play to breathe, so that it draws upon the life which actors and audiences offer to each performance.

The very substance of drama is changeable, and a reader must recognise this fact as much as a dramatist, even though it is more difficult to do so. It is very likely that the reader has never seen actors testing one interpretation against another in rehearsal. Most modern theatres show only productions that are carefully controlled so that they give a clear – and therefore a strong – enactment of a single interpretative idea. At school or university the reader may have been trained to read a text so that he can be sure that he understands precisely what is on the page: whereas he should have been encouraged to play with conjecture and to enter imaginatively within a forever-changing image, or mirage, of another life.

Throughout the twentieth century, critics have reminded their readers that Shakespeare's plays are plays, that this dramatist gave little or no attention to having his texts printed for readers, that words are only part of a performance. But still, even in these latter days, a 'new guide' to Shakespeare is needed because so many earlier aids to study have paid no more than lip-service to the theatrical element in which Shakespeare's works truly and changeably live.

One of the commonest ways of considering the plays 'as if in performance' is to look for visual as well as verbal clues. But the search for 'actions' implicit in the text, in addition to those explicitly required by stage directions, can lay the same dead hand on a play's imaginative life as an exclusive concern for words. It can raise a false dichotomy between speech and gesture, words and show, and prevent any just appraisal of the continuous, complex and coherent human image. Readers who respond in this way may end up clutching a few straws, separate from the play's natural life, just like those who insist that the words of a text are the only reliable (because the only 'fixed') indication of Shakespeare's creation.

Critics who consider the theatrical element of the plays in a wider sense may still experience their own difficulties which are betrayed by vague and sometimes condescending references to particular performances. For example, Harry Levin in his *The Question of Hamlet* (1959) claims that: 'It has taken more bookish Shakespeareans many generations to understand the controlling importance of stage performance' (pp. 131–2). But Professor Levin's attention to theatrical dimensions is no more than incidental to his basic argument. He refers to actual performances to exemplify critical attitudes. Sarah

Bernhardt's Hamlet is said to be part of the 'romantic legend of a weakling, too delicate for this world' (p. 5). Edwin Booth is identified as 'a romantic actor' and is said to be typical of those who found 'congenial' the assumption that 'Hamlet was really the victim of the mental disease he claimed to be simulating' (p. 111). Levin has little time for either of these critical notions and so his theatrical instances are presented only for ridicule. In support of an interpretation he rates more important, he introduces a new paragraph with reference to Tommaso Salvini, and the actor is given a vague puff of commendation: 'one of the most celebrated Hamlets of theatrical history'. We are told he was able to sum up his part 'in a single trait: *il dubbio*' (p. 74). But, having provided this entrance for the theme of doubt, Salvini slips out of the mind of the critic as the latter proceeds with a long quotation from Erasmus who is said to be borrowing from Plato. On each of these occasions a particular theatrical reference has been used, not very precisely, as a kind of exfoliation of a more serious discourse on the play. Each of them could be cut without loss. If this is all Professor Levin can draw from his theatrical knowledge, it is not surprising that the words cited earlier stand thus in fuller quotation:

It has taken more bookish Shakespeareans many generations to understand the controlling importance of stage performance; now that such understanding has been reached, there may be some danger of overemphasis.

Words *versus* action and study *versus* theatre are conflicts that should never be accepted or adjudicated. A reader of Shakespeare is like a performer or an audience, and has no true option but to respond imaginatively to a whole, human and only partly perceived living-image.

The text of each play has to be set in motion in the mind as if it were part of a performance in a theatre. Natural instinct helps, but most readers need to make a conscious effort to do this and they will look around for help. Annotated editions of Shakespeare might seem the most likely recourse, but the principles on which these aids to study have been compiled are indebted so heavily to semantics, literary detection and the pursuit of a definitive text that their footnotes are of little help. Consider, for example, the exchange between Alonso and Prospero, and the latter's charge to Ariel at the conclusion of *The Tempest*:

ALON.   I long
        To hear the story of your life, which must
        Take the ear strangely.

PROS.   I'll deliver all;
And promise you calm seas, auspicious gales,
And sail so expeditious that shall catch
Your royal fleet far off. [*Aside to Ariel*] My Ariel, chick,
That is thy charge. Then to the elements
Be free, and fare thou well! – Please you, draw near.   [*Exeunt*]

I choose this play for illustration because Frank Kermode's edition is
one of the very best of the New Arden series, and the more recent New
Penguin edition by Anne Barton is unusually perceptive. Yet neither
editor pauses for long over these lines because, *as a collection of words*, they
present only a few difficulties.

Professor Kermode picks up *Take* and glosses it 'Affect, captivate'; he
also quotes a parallel usage in *The Winter's Tale*. For *deliver all* he gives a
simple gloss: 'Tell everything'; and for *far off* he offers two possibilities:
'Which is now far off; or: far off as it is.' The grammatical construction of
so expeditious, that rates a longer note:

For this construction, which is not uncommon, see Abbot p[ara.] 279. The
meaning is: I promise you . . . such speedy progress that it will enable you to
overhaul your royal fleet. Cf. v i 17–20.

The note's concluding reference is to Sycorax, Caliban's mother, 'That
could control the moon, make flows and ebbs'. The ideas behind *the
elements* are complex, and here the reader is referred to a special
Appendix B on 'Ariel as Dæmon and Fairy'. Then, except for one word,
'*chick*, the editor's task is done; for this, a simple cross-reference suffices:
'Cf. IV i 184.' Looking up the line yields 'this was well done my bird',
which also has a footnote – "Cf. 'My Ariel, chick', v i 317" – which
sends the reader back to the original problem only a little the wiser.

Although the New Penguin format allows the use of extended
footnotes, Anne Barton is editorially content with '*Take*: captivate' and
'*shall catch/Your royal fleet far off*: enable you to overtake your royal fleet
on the way back to Naples'.

All this editorial comment may be worse than no help at all; it
obscures positively the fact that the passage is loaded with difficulties.
What is the image of life and what may the words do as part of that
image?

Let us look at the concluding line. Prospero says farewell to Ariel and
there is no verbal reply. What does the spirit *do*? Does he fly up and
disappear above the stage? Would this be a repetition of previous
occasions, or does he fly more quickly or more slowly than before? Does
he fly in a vertical or a lateral direction? Does he laugh 'merrily', as he
had promised in his song (v i 88–94)? Or does he smile, before he
moves away? Or do his face and his whole body remain immobile for a

brief moment (there is no *exit* marked in the only Jacobean text we have of the play) and, if so, how soon does he leave, and in what way? Or is Ariel convulsed with life before moving away to become 'free'? Perhaps, like Keats's 'young Apollo', he should 'shriek' the moment he has left the stage, as all his limbs find perfect life.

And what does Prospero do? At this moment I have seen Prosperos fighting back their tears, others weeping helplessly, and some turning abruptly away. The magician-duke may have never so much as looked at Ariel during the whole play, but this spirit has 'cleaved' to his thoughts and is now called 'My Ariel, chick': the last word a term of endearment to a young child and closely related (if not identical) to 'chuck' which Shakespeare had used several times in other plays between lovers and comrades. The experienced actor of Prospero will have relied on the support of the young actor of Ariel throughout the play at moments of great excitement, grandeur and anger; and he has just shared its most crucial and delicate moment with him, waiting for the boy to give his cue:

> ARIEL . . .   Your charm so strongly works 'em
> That if you now beheld them your affections
> Would become tender.
> PROS.   Dost think so, spirit?
> ARIEL Mine would, sir, were I human.
> PROS.   And mine shall. . . .   (v i 17–20)

At the end of the play, in this moment of farewell, two actors in two such roles, who have shared such a tender and deep understanding, cannot part without their very different performances giving some indication of their common achievement. Feeling may be variously expressed at this point, but never totally hidden.

The dramatic crux that exists between two short sentences in the last line of the play –

> Be free, and fare thou well! – Please you, draw near.

– must be recognised by every reader of the text. No stage-direction is there to warn him, and no editorial note; but he must imagine the moment in living terms and in the context of the whole play, especially in the light of the two performances until this moment. So received, as part of an image of life, the words themselves become potent, beyond literary belief.

This does not mean that literary qualities are no longer relevant to a reader, but rather that words will come under a new scrutiny. The rhythms of Prospero's speech are of crucial importance; the structure of his thought and the metrical form —

> ...   My Ariel, chick,
> That is thy charge.   ...

— would be wholly different if 'chick' were not placed at a line-end, if the possessive pronoun were missing, or if the demonstrative and inclusive 'That' did not start the message and imply so neatly that Prospero knows that Ariel has been silently attentive all the while, on the brink of freedom. However Prospero has spoken before this, and whatever the parting means for him now, the shape, weight and music of his words suggest that he speaks with intimate carefulness and self-control. Somewhere, between the two short sentences or even held within the hesitating rhythms that the syntax provides, or when all has been said, Prospero parts from Ariel and the full drama is realised.

Then Prospero, sometimes in command of himself and sometimes broken and exhausted, turns to his friends and enemies. Does he look at all of them in the same way? Or are his eyes half closed, or fixed at some distant object? How quickly does he turn? Does 'draw near' imply that he stands still as they all file past him and into the cell which had been the centre of his secret life? Does the treacherous Antonio go in last, and, if so, how do the brothers face each other? Prospero had said

> ...   They being penitent
> The sole drift of my purpose doth extend
> Not a frown further.   ...   (v i 28–30)

But Antonio is *not* penitent.

Much will depend on whether the courtiers have all been 'spell-stopped' while Prospero has spoken to Ariel. This is the easiest way of handling the aside and there is precedent earlier in the scene. Then the courtiers will all break into life again, taking the earlier cue of Prospero's magic promise of auspicious calm and haste. But, then, how fully does the usurped Duke of Milan himself regain that earlier mood, and how soon? On this occasion the talk between master and spirit may have been heard by the others, and then Prospero's guests will hardly know how to move — leave alone speak — until they have had time to respond to 'Pray you, draw near'.

Does Prospero's face show gladness or sadness, when all eyes must be on him? Those two descriptions cannot begin to define the great range of possibilities that lie before an actor. And, this time, the literary qualities of the text — those four simple words being a whole speech in themselves — can yield little certain guidance, beyond polite and measured brevity. Do the other characters move slowly or eagerly, with quickening or fading physical rhythms? Are their movements formal or informal? Do they talk or make other contacts between themselves as they gather together? Do they crowd round Prospero and the entrance to his cell, or do their ordered and splendid ranks dissolve slowly in absolute silence with no apparent difficulty, as if a dream were fading? How long does all this take, and how do the rhythms of this *exeunt* answer and complete the rhythms of the preceding passage and of the movements and sounds of the whole play? Is the subsequent return of Prospero to speak an Epilogue a surprise, rhythmically and visually, or does it appear to be a necessary resolution to the play itself?

There can be few other plays which end with a single speech of four such simple words, especially after such sustained, though falling, rhythms as those of Prospero's two previous longer speeches. I do not think that the monosyllables can be spoken without strong feeling. Has all rancour and sense of personal loss now vanished in an aloof mood of acceptance? Only twenty lines earlier Prospero had dismissed Caliban with a tight-phrased 'Go to: away!'; his invitation here at the conclusion marks a huge transition from that previous dismissal. Is this short speech loud or quiet, quick or slow, spoken with a slight hesitation after two words or as a single premeditated phrase? A reader of the text must recognise how many questions lie behind the words, and ask why Shakespeare has given his play a conclusion that is at once so enigmatic and so open to different subtleties of performance and acceptance.

The difficulty of writing about a theatrical moment is that so much detail is necessary; and always it will be inadequate. The perceptions, represented by a halting catalogue of possibilities, have each come quickly and filled like sails to take the mind forward, down the wind and across it. The expression of this process of exploration in a series of questions is also formally inappropriate. Each query would be better expressed as a probe, a movement outwards into the theatrical possibilities of the text.

That is how an actor works in rehearsal: always he must be positive; he must act. He may stop half-way through or, when the text has all been spoken, he may decide that his direction had been false. But his attempt to make the drama live is for real, a full imaginative committal, not an idle fancy or half-hearted experiment.

The play, as it *might* be, is always within our grasp, if as readers we are ready to move on from each momentary perception towards fuller imaginative possession of the whole. This process can be helped by keeping note of progress and collecting questions, because in this way we retain for a little what we have found, and may keep our wits about us until ready to move on into interplay once more.

Reading a play is not a continuous process, like reading a traditional novel. No clear narrative line is offered, because neither leading character nor author can take full charge of what we must imagine. There is no single point of view. We have to move warily backwards and forwards, as we create for ourselves the living image and begin to explore it. We have to assemble the pieces of dialogue provided in the printed kit, and then supply, as best we can, the imagined realities which alone make theatrical sense of the unspoken words that have been provided. When the drama is afoot on the stage of our minds, the text with which we began will be transformed, and it will never quite fit back on to the page from which we first unpacked it.

A useful rule for a student of Shakespeare is that the text will not stay still, and that he can never *quote* from a play. The words can be reproduced in printed form, but their living interplay in the drama is another matter, one belonging to a different element. Many words more will be needed before the text, once it is alive, can be reproduced in verbal description; and then all will be inadequate.

This does not mean that Shakespeare's words that have survived in printed books are devalued or disregarded in the theatre. Quite the contrary: nowhere are the words and sounds and syntax and suggestions of the printed text so turned over and over in a process of enquiry as they are in the theatre. Actors study them again and again; they learn them by heart and live with them; they grow in imagination and executive power by means of them.

It is easy enough to stop this process and give the public a reading of the text which is based on some momentary insight: many performances do seem to disregard the most obvious directions of the text; all of them have their limitations. But time brings its own corrections; the next attempt to perform the play will be different, and more of the text's theatrical life will have been discovered, absorbed and recreated. There is no 'danger' of belittling Shakespeare's plays by emphasising the 'controlling importance of stage performance'.

The process of discovery, natural to an actor, is available to a reader. It is as natural as breathing, and as inviting as an opportunity to find a world made new or to make contact with the inner experience of the man called Shakespeare. The limitations are our own, and this book will try to show that many of these may be overcome.

3 | Contemporary Shakespeare

One prime difficulty of reading or performing Shakespeare's plays has not so far been mentioned. As a man born in 1564, his mind, environment and expectations, were all different from ours. The language he spoke was in some respects different too, and the ways in which men wrote it. Time has put barriers between then and now.

In Shakespeare's days, kings were absolute rulers, by divine right as well as in actual power; church-going was compulsory; the printed word was strictly censored. Marriage brought personal independence as well as widening responsibilities, but most people had to wait until their mid or later twenties before they could undertake it; and by that age more than half of their life-expectation had gone. Prowess in battle, obedience to a lord or master, subjugation of wife to husband, exercises of piety, education through memorisation, were all highly prized norms. Punishment by death for a number of offences was upheld as morally and socially necessary. Universal suffrage, equal opportunity, racial equality, religious tolerance, bureaucratic control, psychiatry, contraception, were all either unknown or highly suspect. Hardly any statement about morality, society, politics or psychology that we might make today would be comprehensible to Shakespeare's contemporaries. And, if we think at all deeply about what words imply, the same is true the other way round. Elizabethans had different thoughts, and deployed them in different ways, from us. The more we read their books and study the surviving records, the more aware we become of the distance between them and us, and the difficulty of understanding all that Shakespeare's words imply.

The changes that time has brought are more apparent in other arts. The strict formality that governed Elizabethan music we recognise at once. The painters of that age can be seen to be bound by tradition, and its architects to be seeking to base their art on classical rules and proportions with the obviousness of beginners. Structural complications of scholastic rhetoric and the accumulation of authorities and ornament are often more conspicuous in prose publications than in dramatic dialogue; but we have only to remember how natural it is for modern dramatists to write in prose for the different conventions of Shakespeare's theatre to thrust themselves forward for attention. In those days the first, almost unquestioned, choice was to write plays in verse, and rhyme and rhetorical elaboration were not uncommon. Elizabethan taste, education and conditions of composition profoundly affected the plays of Shakespeare, to a degree that only a developed historical understanding – and one that takes account of the large social and intellectual changes that were becoming more apparent as each year passed – can begin to comprehend. Men who sought security in the standards of the past began to despair of the age and of their fellow men. The new grammar schools, established earlier in the century, sent pupils out into the world with mental horizons far wider than those of their parents. Shakespeare was one such pupil. Newly acquired skills and personal initiatives modified society at every level. New money challenged the value of territorial inheritance and, at the same time, bands of unemployed homeless people lived and died as fugitives, with almost no rights in law. The *Discours de la Méthode* by René Descartes, published in 1637, was perhaps the most powerful single agent in eventually opening all intellectual, moral and religious ideas to scientific investigation; but already, by the time Shakespeare wrote *Hamlet*, around the year 1600, pragmatism and scepticism were governing the thoughts and deeds of many, in conflict with the older guides of tradition and authority. A new sense of man, society and history was emerging.

Open the works of Edmund Spenser, Sir Philip Sidney or Sir Walter Ralegh (each born a dozen or less years before Shakespeare), or those of Christopher Marlowe (born the same year as Shakespeare) or of John Donne (born eight years later), and you will quickly come upon a passage that needs careful exegesis before any adequate meaning can be discerned. In form, theme, style, argument and reference, these writings are often obscure for us. We feel much more at home in Shakespeare's plays, but that is only because we are familiar with them. We must remember that they are also a product of those times, and we must make an act of historical restoration if our understanding is not to be clouded or out of true focus.

However, I want to leave to a later stage considering Shakespeare in his own age, and instead emphasise at this point an important difference between his works and those of most of his contemporaries. The fact is that his plays are more alive today than any other writings from that time. So direct can be our enjoyment that we need to be alerted to the changes that time has brought and the meanings, subtleties and colours that have become obscured. If we ask why this should be, we may recognise Shakespeare's distinctive achievement and be able to develop our response along the most direct and unimpeded course.

☆

As early as 1623, one of Shakespeare's contemporaries recognised his indestructibility:

> Triumph, my Britain, thou hast one to show
> To whom all scenes of Europe homage owe.
> He was not of an age, but for all time!   . . .

The last line runs confidently and has become a commonplace, but Ben Jonson did not write facile literary panegyrics. As a classicist he knew the significance of the claims he made in these verses prefixed to the first collected edition of Shakespeare's plays. He marshalled all known Greek and Roman dramatists for comparison, as well as John Lyly, Thomas Kyd and Christopher Marlowe, his older contemporaries. Jonson's bardolatry was deliberate:

> And all the Muses still were in their prime
> When like Apollo he came forth to warm
> Our ears, or like a Mercury to charm.   . . .

Shakespeare was the 'star of poets' – in the sense that the king in *Henry V* was the 'star of England' (Epilogue, 6) – without whose 'rage or influence' the London stage had no hope of survival.

In the eyes of the younger dramatists, the reason why Shakespeare's works were pre-eminent and timeless was that he was the truest of poets. If we listen to Jonson, who knew Shakespeare very well, and worked for the same theatre and same public, it will be the poetic qualities of the plays that we will seek out first when we try to read them from the distance of our own age.

This does not mean that we should forget that we are reading plays and not poems, or that Jonson valued Shakespeare's sonnets and narrative verse above his dramas. The terms 'dramatist' and 'playwright' were unknown in England at that time, and did not enter the language until the end of the seventeenth century – a neat example of the changes which time has made to the language that are not immediately noticeable to a modern reader. Elizabethans who wrote plays were called, commonly, writers and authors or, in derogation, scribblers and 'rascally rhymers'. Only special qualities entitled them to the grand name of poet.

Ben Jonson often wrote and talked about this 'high calling', and he spent his life trying to follow it:

First, we require in our poet or maker – for that title our language affords him elegantly with the Greek – a goodness of natural wit. For whereas all other arts consist of doctrine and precepts, the poet must be able, by nature and instinct, to pour out the treasure of his mind; . . . the poetic rapture. . . . Then it riseth higher, as by a divine instinct, when it contemns common and known conceptions. It utters somewhat above a mortal mouth. Then it gets aloft, and flies away with his rider, whither before it was doubtful to ascend. This the poets understood by their Helicon, Pegasus, or Parnassus.[1]

'Sacred invention' was the 'peculiar food' of poetry, and the name of 'true poet' was the greatest adornment of humanity – so said young Knowell to his father in Jonson's *Every Man in his Humour* (1598), and Shakespeare must have heard this speech very often because he acted in the play and probably took the part of the young poet's father. In conversation, Jonson confessed that he himself was possessed by such imaginary activity. He could be

. . . oppressed with fantasy, which hath ever mastered his reason; a general disease in many poets. . . .

He hath consumed a whole night in lying looking to his great toe, about which he hath seen Tartars and Turks, Romans and Carthaginians, fight in his imagination.[2]

Shakespeare, too, believed that a poet must have a strong imagination, although he made less boast of the matter. He gave Duke Theseus, in *A Midsummer Night's Dream*, the most to say on the subject. He starts by claiming that what the poet writes is 'more strange than true' and that his 'seething brains' and 'shaping fantasies' will

> . . .   apprehend
> More than cool reason ever comprehends.   . . .   (v i 5–6)

But it is significant that Theseus goes beyond Jonson and likens the poet to both lunatic and enraptured lover:

> The lunatic, the lover, and the poet,
> Are of imagination all compact.
> One sees more devils than vast hell can hold:
> That is the madman. The lover, all as frantic,
> Sees Helen's beauty in a brow of Egypt.
> The poet's eye, in a fine frenzy rolling,
> Doth glance from heaven to earth, from earth to heaven;

> And as imagination bodies forth
> The forms of things unknown, the poet's pen
> Turns them to shapes, and gives to airy nothing
> A local habitation and a name.
> Such tricks hath strong imagination
> That, if it would but apprehend some joy,
> It comprehends some bringer of that joy.   . . .   (7–20)

In Shakespeare's day, the word 'frenzy' – however clearly and perhaps ironically linked with 'fine' – described the last outrages of madness, an uncontrollable state of unreason, beyond the merely 'frantic'. Theseus sums up by saying that the poet might just as well be living in darkness:

> . . . in the night, imagining some fear,
> How easy is a bush suppos'd a bear.

As Hippolyta his bride points out, the paradox is that fancy's images can grow

> . . . to something of great constancy,
> But howsoever strange and admirable.   (v i 26–7)

Shakespeare has used much the same concepts as Jonson, and developed them in his own way. For him, the poet rides aloft on the Pegasus of his imagination, and gives precise verbal form to the strange and yet true creatures of his fantasies.

In the Prologue for *Henry V*, Shakespeare's Chorus speaks for both poet and actors:

> O for a Muse of fire, that would ascend
> The brightest heaven of invention,
> A kingdom for a stage, princes to act,
> And monarchs to behold the swelling scene.   . . .   (Prol. 1–4)

He flatters and encourages his audience, but he is also preparing them for the drama, an ideal play that outstrips reality. Like Jonson, he sees 'invention' ascending to a bright heaven; but then he calls on the 'imaginary forces' of the spectators to share the adventure, and transform the weak efforts of poet and actors into a more dazzling, frightening and astounding experience. The audience, as the Chorus says elsewhere, must 'entertain conjecture' and so realise in their imaginations a horrid battle, or the vast darkness and subtle noises of a watchful night. Poet, actors and audience must all allow the play to live in their fantasies.

In a very early play, *The Two Gentlemen of Verona*, there is further talk of the 'force of heaven-bred poesy', only this time Shakespeare has his character insist that its strange attraction is not all from the head. The very 'sinews' of a poet are vital parts of the instrument on which he plays:

> For Orpheus' lute was strung with poet's sinews,
> Whose golden touch could soften steel and stones,
> Make tigers tame, and huge leviathans
> Forsake unsounded deeps to dance on sands.   . . . (III ii 78–81)

His hearers think themselves transformed, and leave their usual elements to achieve the impossible, however briefly or absurdly.

Quite simply, Shakespeare was the most imaginative of poets: the imaginary world that he possessed in his mind and expressed in his writing was more alive, potent, deeply founded and finely considered than that of his fellows. He was the 'star of poets', and for that reason his works outlive his own time and are more immediately accessible to us than those of his contemporaries.

☆

The common ground, where we can meet freely with Shakespeare, is not to be sought in what Jonson called 'doctrine and precepts'. We should never begin by asking what every word means, or what a play means, or whether we know its argument. If we start by trying to nail down what the drama is saying, we shall never rise with the poet's invention and enter the strange world of his plays.

Of course meanings abound and our minds are set to work. Shakespeare delighted in creating kings, full of royal thoughts and obsessed with power; and we have to respond as 'monarchs' if we are to 'behold the swelling scene' with fitting imagination. The interests and tensions of 'warlike Harry', the cunning of political operators on both sides of the war in France, the superstitions of innkeepers and foot-soldiers, are all brought into play in *Henry V* along with subtleties of language. But the essential fact to grasp is that meanings – verbal statements or definitive gestures – never work alone: a man's mind is only part of his being, and argument is only part of a play's life.

If Shakespeare's history plays depended on political or moral argument, they would not be vital today. Economic, social, intellectual and technological changes have altered the very basis of our concerns. For us providence, order, authority, responsibility and the nature of good and evil, all raise problems of understanding that Shakespeare could never have known or guessed. But we still dream of new possessions; we are still parents, sons and daughters; we feel pain, hardship and weariness; we exercise power and submit to it; we know about preparations for conflict, about responsibility and irresponsibility, about uncertainty, terrors of the night, violence, cruelty, guilt, and the upsurge of joy as dangers are passed. We know, too, how men and women speak and are speechless, and how they may be divided or brought together by a quick instinct for aggression, laughter or sexual response. In the presentation of all this and much more, *The Chronicle History of Henry the Fifth* lives today.

The primacy of imagination in Shakespeare's plays does not mean that they are mindless or that 'doctrine and precepts' did not concern their author. It has been said that Shakespeare had no opinions of his own because he let his characters say whatever the story required and left the audience to judge which was right or wrong. A twentieth-century dramatist, Edward Bond, has denounced that shallow conclusion:

Had Shakespeare not spent his creative life desperately struggling to reconcile problems that obsessed him, he could not have written with such intellectual strength and passionate beauty. What were these problems? The nature of right and wrong, in what way an individual should be part of his society, why some men are tyrants and others nearly saints, why some governments are despotic and why at other times reason appears briefly to rule a country or a city. He asked these questions as he passed from youth to age in a world that was both young and old.[3]

Shakespeare did explore the boundaries of his own knowledge, but in plays, not in treatises, formal methods of speculation or manifestoes. His imagination created an image of life to be enacted within the time and place of performance, and his 'opinions' about any subject can be represented only by what happens in that imaginary world. As readers or performers of his plays, we have to make that world live in our consciousness, using whatever our experience, 'natural wit' and imagination can bring to that adventure.

The range and variety of the characters in Shakespeare's plays show the huge reach of his concerns for social life; the articulation of their plots expresses an analytical restlessness and a search for correspondences and comparisons. The sequence of his plays, in all the variety of setting, form and mood, charts the course of his passionate and responsible thought. He wrestled with images of men and women, with relationships between them, and with the cause and effect of actions. He pursued conclusions to which he could give different kinds of assent, and sometimes he had to bring a play to an end with some cry of helplessness or act of supernatural or accidental intervention.

The breed of imaginary human beings that Shakespeare wrought so carefully and magnificently carries with it many ideas, clichés, crude pronouncements and intricate verbal definitions, but each individual has his fuller being and just appraisal in the world of total performance, in which nothing human is disregarded and everything comes into the reckoning. The early history plays were followed by tragedies and harsh comedies, with their own *dramatis personæ*:

> No one before Shakespeare [Bond observes] had looked so closely at the human mind and the passions, fears and hopes raging in it. And not one of these individuals could have fitted into the society of the good government he had spent so long in describing and praising in the history plays. His honesty makes him reject his first explanations.[4]

The energy of Shakespeare's imagination was matched by an enquiring, responsible mind, which expressed itself in plays for performance.

We can enter those plays wherever our imagination is caught, and then, as in a waking dream, we must follow as if the shadow were substantial; we must be ready for all that is encountered, in the form of each individual play and the ordering of each sentence of its dialogue. The exciting sense of freedom which we experience is that of imaginative co-operation, not an absence of controlling form or a casualness of thought. We are free to discover the look in a character's eye, the pressure of a hand, the pitch of voice or the movement of one honest man through a group of conspirators. Such effects are not disfigured by the passing of time. Everyone can bring experience and dreams into the encounter, and so set hopes and fears at hazard. It is an open and endless engagement.

So Shakespeare is alive for our time, and not restricted to his own age. As well as in the larger elements of character, action and spectacle, this is true for each brief moment. Imagination is at work in a single line or phrase: each movement of a hand or an eye can be both 'strange and true'.

Jonson knew very well that imagination had to be allied with understanding and craft, and that silliest ignorance, blind affection and chance had no part in a play's life. Although a poet's 'matter' depends upon natural quickness of invention, everything has to be justly fashioned. A poet who attempts to 'cast to write a living line must sweat', Jonson declares,

>   . . .   and strike the second heat
> Upon the Muses' anvil; turn the same,
> And himself with it, that he thinks to frame;

> Or, for the laurel, he may gain a scorn,
> For a good poet's made, as well as born;
> And such wert thou. Look how the father's face
> Lives in his issue; even so, the race
> Of Shakespeare's mind and manners brightly shines
> In his well-turnéd and true-filéd lines;   . . .
>   ('To . . . William Shakespeare')

The result is that we can stop reading a play and hold a few words in our minds for days on end. The lines of dialogue have been so turned and struck on the Muses' anvil – and Shakespeare's 'own self' with them – that they are wrought and compacted with imaginative invention. Almost never do the words express a definitive or one-dimensional statement. The whole imaginative experience of a play in action was at work, deep down, in the creation of a single line. Half-a-dozen words can suggest several levels of consciousness in the speaker's mind and in the minds of the audience; they may reverberate and echo from one scene to another. A speech can never be prised out of its context without loss or falsification; the very sound of its being spoken at the appropriate moment in a performance is part of its life.

If we give our closest, direct attention to Shakespeare's dialogue, it can activate our senses, without our conscious and time-conditioned knowledge. We seem to see, hear and touch; and to move with the characters who speak. We can be caught up into a dynamic imaginative life that draws on an everyday experience common to us and the poet's contemporaries:

> To be, or not to be – that is the question;
> Whether 'tis nobler in the mind to suffer
> The slings and arrows of outrageous fortune,
> Or to take arms against a sea of troubles,
> And by opposing end them? To die, to sleep:
> No more; and by a sleep to say we end
> The heart-ache and the thousand natural shocks
> That flesh is heir to. 'Tis a consummation
> Devoutly to be wished. . . .   (*Hamlet*, III i 56–64)

Hamlet, more than most of Shakespeare's characters, is interested in the very quiddities of words; he quotes them, repeats them and reads them. Here he questions his own thoughts. But the speech starts simply with monosyllables of everyday occurrence; a broken rhythm marks the intellectual effort of definition, and then that mental action is sustained by a more fluent affirmation. With the start of the second line, the speech is afloat on a longer phrase, running for two full lines but detonated suddenly, half-way through, with 'slings and arrows'. As we read, speak or listen imaginatively, our senses seem to be struck by weapons that are swift, sudden and piercing; and as we respond to this physical image, a battle starts in the mind, dangerous and cruel. Perhaps the word 'suffer' has already betrayed the entrance of particular and physical sensation underneath the progress of abstract thought.

Hamlet's mind and senses work fully now, and words are pulled to and fro in many ways. For Shakespeare, 'outrageous' was associated with the violence and noise of madness, as well as with battle, crime and immorality; and so the abstract concept of 'fortune' is humanised or personalised in frightening form. Speaker and hearer may now cringe with fear or hesitate with loss of distinct focus. Then the speech makes a new and more deliberate movement:

> Or to take arms against a sea of troubles .

The image of a battle is continued in the idea of taking up 'arms', but these words also suggest a slower, more individual and determined physical action. And, in the very same line, the word 'sea' changes the mental picture to a wide and inhuman expanse of deep water. 'Troubles' is less precise and so the associations with death that 'sea' will often have in our dreams may also register on a deeper, more pervasive level. The verb 'end' carries such thoughts further towards the surface of consciousness, and then on to 'die' and 'sleep'. Syntax is abrupt now, and rhythms broken. The speech stops and the underlying thoughts seem to draw back. Hamlet is aware of himself speaking as others do: he looks for fulfilment and recognises peaceful wishes.

The speaking of such lines involves an actor in imaginative exploration and changing mental and physical awareness. In slow motion we can work out something of their progress in the white-hot forge where Shakespeare struck on the 'Muses' anvil'; and in performance we can identify imaginatively, according to our own individual minds and experience, with Hamlet's confrontation of his situation.

In chapters 7 and 8 we will consider in greater detail how we should respond to Shakespeare's 'living lines'. Here it is sufficient to notice that, however philosophical or political, however topical, complicated or learned are the words that Shakespeare's characters may speak, our task in reading or performing is, basically, an imaginative act which must draw upon our own twentieth-century experience. Queen Cleopatra, dressed in splendid and ancient robes, feels a common 'pinch' and breathes in the 'soft' air of ordinary day (*A. & C.*, v ii 293, 309). Richard the Second, associating himself with the 'glistering Phaethon' of ancient mythology and literary tradition, also fastens on the simple action of 'Down, down I come', repeating the elements of this phrase

with a dramatic and musical emphasis that indicates gestures and actions for any man at any time; and then, suddenly, he hears, in his fantasy, the shriek of a 'night-owl' and the high, remote song of 'larks' (*R. II*, III iii 178–83).

Shakespeare's words ask us to respond with alacrity of mind, freedom of imagination or fantasy, and the touch of everyday experience. As Theseus implies in *A Midsummer Night's Dream*, however fierce the 'bear' which the drama presents, the quality of a very ordinary 'bush' is part of the means that created it and must re-create it in our minds.

☆

In imagination we can enter Shakespeare's plays despite the obscurities that time has brought; and we can possess them as extensions of our own individual lives. In this way we are free within the drama's reality, co-operating in re-creation. We can also be possessed by a play until our minds turn reeling from the illusion; we can find what we could never expect and confront those selves to which we are always strangers.

The plays are 'strange' as well as 'true'. Most obviously, they are set in foreign countries or ancient times. The earliest written are located in Rome of the fourth century AD, or in 'the pleasant garden of great Italy', or in Ephesus, or in England before the Tudor dynasty had been established. Even if Shakespeare had wished to set them in his own here-and-now, he would not have been allowed to do so. A royal edict forbade any theatrical performance 'wherein either matters of religion or of the governance of the estate of the commonweal shall be handled or treated'; to do so would be construed as treasonous, and the penalties were severe. England was a police state and only authority's voice was free to pronounce on the state of the land or the peace of men's minds: the crowded, excitable theatres were kept under strict surveillance. The only way a writer could escape censure was to avoid writing about any one who was alive. Ministers of religion in Shakespeare's plays are therefore papal legates to the ruler, friars of no fixed theology, a 'churlish priest', 'kind father' or 'lady Abbess', none of whom could have authority in Elizabethan England. Harry of Monmouth, 'plume-pluck'd Richard', Caesar and 'noble Brutus' were all dead and could not contest their dramatic representation. Matters of 'religion' or of 'governance' are everywhere in Shakespeare's plays, as they are in life, but always transposed into some fictive world so that they may be shown in their own true colours and escape punitive censure.

This may well have been Shakepeare's own preference, for the further he carried his explorations of man and society, the greater distance he set between them and the present time, his own country and living persons. The great tragedies are located in primitive Denmark –

the story of Hamlet was first written down in the twelfth century – and in a land of thanes and elected kings, in ancient Rome or Athens, in pagan Britain and the 'free state' of Venice where an infidel could thrive in business and a Moor lead an army. Within these plays, the action moves from human habitations to a 'blasted heath' where witches meet or into the full force of the 'to-and-fro conflicting wind and rain'. Characters go on strange journeys where they encounter pirates who are 'thieves of mercy' or escape shipwreck on the 'enchaféd flood'. The last comedies are set in the most exotic lands of all, and their narratives work most strongly in the 'level' of our dreams.

Even in the earliest plays, the heroes move progressively towards uncharted experience. In *Richard III* this takes the form of a nightmare in which the tyrant's victims rise from the dead to curse him and bless his adversary. In *Richard II* the fantasy is not so blatant but, when the king is in prison and alone with his own thoughts, the dramatist has provided, against all likelihood, an unseen and unnamed character to play music off-stage, suitably out of time. Then a groom of the royal stable enters who has got permission to tell how Bolingbroke 'rode on roan Barbary' (v vi 78) and how the animal had carried his new master 'so proudly as if he disdain'd the ground'. It is at this precise moment that Richard's murderers are preparing to enter. The end of *Henry V* is possibly more surprising, although here Shakespeare had full historical warranty for the event if not the manner of its enactment. The dramatist decided to place the king in strange waters, and so he dismissed the whole French and English courts from the stage, and left Henry to encounter the young French princess, Katherine, in a language she does not understand or, alternatively, in one that he does not understand. The warrior-king is out of his depth – earnest, insecure and laughable by turns. When they kiss at last, Henry says that there is 'witchcraft' in that moment's physical intimacy and silence (v ii 272).

At the end of the comedies, fantasy and transformations are often the sole means of concluding the action. In *As You Like It*, Rosalind announces that she can do 'strange things' (v ii 52); and after a musical interlude about 'a lover and his lass', a spirit appears from nowhere: no word of the play has prepared for a supernatural character, but now the young god Hymen enters with his train and they sing:

> Then is there mirth in heaven
> When earthly things made even
>   Atone together.   . . .   (v iv 102 ff.)

The conclusions of some of the comedies are so fantastic that they recall the 'fierce vexation of a dream'.[5]

In *The Comedy of Errors* the improbabilities are fast and furious. The

Duke says, 'I think you all have drunk of Circe's cup . . .' and, a moment later, 'I think you are all mated or stark mad' (v i 270 & 281). Such final fantasy does not signal a carefree and facile release from all human concerns, but a further and more dangerous voyage for the principal characters.

All the tragic heroes come close to madness. At certain times irrational diatribes and passionate simplicities of cruelty, violence and suffering are all that the plays offer. But the action moves on and the poet continues to 'frame' the strange visions that his 'eye' had seen in the 'frenzy' of his imagination. In this way the heroes reveal their deepest resources.

In *Macbeth* Caithness and Angus are at hand to chart the usurper's course:

> c.   Some say he's mad; others, that lesser hate him,
>   Do call it valiant fury; but for certain
>   He cannot buckle his distemper'd cause
>   Within the belt of rule.
> A.   Now does he feel
>   His secret murders sticking on his hands;   . . . (v ii 13–17)

Until now Macbeth had understood and commanded his fury:

> Though you untie the winds and let them fight
> Against the churches; though the yesty waves
> Confound and swallow navigation up;
> Though bladed corn be lodg'd and trees blown down;
> Though castles topple on their warders' heads;
> Though palaces and pyramids do slope
> Their heads to their foundations; though the treasure
> Of nature's germens tumble all together,
> Even till destruction sicken – answer me
> To what I ask you.   (iv i 52–61)

When he had returned to the witches and spoken these words, Macbeth was still terribly sane, in full control of a vision of desolation. It is nearer the end when other thoughts of idiocy, darkness, senselessness and irrationality bring him to the edge of consciousness and into madness. It is then that he leaps forward in wrath and desperately seeks to draw together his wits and strength for a final resolution. Fear, weariness and regret alternate helplessly with furious action, and he draws destruction upon himself:

> Ring the alarum bell. Blow wind, come wrack;
> At least we'll die with harness on our back.   (v v 51–2)

A nightmare life-in-death continues and it tests every human resource. But when Macduff taunts him as a 'rarer monster', Macbeth determines, clearly and with fullest committal, that he will 'try the last' in a wordless fight (v viii 32). Then, too late for dissimulation or vacillation, he must reveal his last resource of valour.

As we read, perform or watch the plays, we must journey imaginatively into the unknown, responding to their total actions as best we may. So we are raised on the poet's Pegasus. The final destination is neither clearly signposted nor, still less, wholly described.

When King Lear believes that he and Cordelia can become 'God's spies' – 'And take upon's the mystery of things' (v iii 16–17) – the tragedy is not finished. The old king, of more than eighty years, has yet to see his daughter hanged and, in the struggle, to kill her executioner. Then he has to rejoin the survivors of his terrible actions and fail to make coherent sense. Does he die in hope because he believes that Cordelia is alive, or is the absolute knowledge of her death the last turn upon life's rack for his suffering being? When does Lear die? Does he make any response to Edgar? How is his pain made visible? Shakespeare has defined precisely the context in which Lear endures his last moments, but the heart of his experience cannot be given a name or 'local habitation': it is not containable. The end of the play, in all its strangeness and truth, is the product of nothing less than the whole imaginative and feelingly lifelike adventure of its performance, and it can be defined in no simpler terms.

Prospero in *The Tempest* is a magician who can summon innumerable and subtle spirits to 'enact his present fancies' (iv i 121–2). The masque-like illusions that result include a terrifying harpy, that claps its wings before denouncing 'three men of sin', and furious hounds that chase foolish conspirators. All these are potent and irresistible. But the vision which presents the richness of a world at peace, and is conjured into being for the delight of the magician's only daughter and her prince, is interrupted by the creator himself. It vanishes with discordant noise, while Prospero is so torn by passion that Miranda declares she has never seen her father 'with anger so distemper'd' (iv i 145). This is in keeping with Shakespeare's creative mind which was never wholly content in giving easy pleasure or delivering a clear message. His fantasy offered no escape from life, and no rest. Perhaps Hamlet speaks also for his creator in saying of himself

> O God, I could be bounded in a nutshell and count myself a king of infinite space, were it not that I have bad dreams.   (ii ii 254–5)

Shakespeare experienced and gave form to a perpetually waking dream, and our understanding is teased to say what that dream means:

'There is no man that can tell what',[6] not even the poet himself. The most we know is that Shakespeare's plays have continued to engage other imaginations and by that means to have contemporary life. For us, in a very different world from his, the enchantment is still potent whenever we explore Shakespeare's lifelike image of life with our own imagination.

4 | *Parts for Actors*

In his mind, as he writes or rewrites a play, a dramatist takes all the parts himself. If he has been an actor, the imagined performances will be detailed and precise. If he has had a hand in casting, production or management, he may envisage, at some stage in composition, the whole process of rehearsal and something of the final test of performance. Shakespeare, who was both actor and manager, must have experienced all this very keenly. He knew that his script would be realised by fellow members of the Chamberlain's Men – or after the death of Elizabeth I, the King's Men – and so he would be more able than most modern dramatists to set the play in action in his own mind. The performers of his play would be men whom he knew very well from daily and creative contact. Their individual rhythms and voices, the pitch, pressures, excitements and tricks of their characteristic performances, their varied experience and imaginative reach, would all be somewhere in his consciousness as he wrote, and would mingle, from time to time, with the imaginary men and women whom he created for the fictions of his plays.

Such complications could inhibit a lesser writer, but Shakespeare thrived on them. Incidental images and some favourite theatrical words show that actors were seldom far from his mind as he worked. His scripts have proved to be very practical from an actor's point of view, and very demanding and rewarding as well. For nearly four centuries they have attracted and challenged performers in many different kinds of theatre and in many languages. Great actors have found their early successes in Shakespeare's plays, and developed their individual talents by return-ing to them again and again throughout their careers.

In Elizabethan theatres, a writer had more need to understand the actor's art than he does today, because there was then no director to interpret and present his work for audiences. On the open, platform stage, which was found in all the public theatres, actors had to gain attention for themselves, right from the start of a performance, and then hold it. The stage was like a three-sided boxing-ring and theatres were

31

built on much the same plan as bull-baiting arenas. For most of the time the actors stood at the centre of the circled auditorium, high above many of the spectators; they were truly on their own, without much support from the background of the tiring-house façade and without any special scenic or lighting effects. They encountered their audience in the same daylight that lit the stage, and they had to offset any diversion that might arise from talk between neighbours in the auditorium, vocal comments on the performance and the continuous sale of food and drink. They had to counteract the impatience and movements of the crowds who stood in the theatre yard to see the show. In Elizabethan days, the actors had to rule. Thomas Dekker, a dramatist of the next generation after Shakespeare's, said that an audience was like a great beast which the actors, with the dramatist's help, had to tame into silence and attention.

These conditions of performance ensured that it was the actors who became popular attractions; they were at the centre of any successful theatre enterprise. In Shakespeare's company, they chose the repertoire and decided the casting; they were part-owners of the theatres in which they performed and were in charge of every activity; and they kept most of the money for themselves. Anyone can recognise the vitality of Shakespeare's writing simply by reading a text, as if a play were just another book with a story, and characters and argument to present. But to understand the dynamics and subtleties of his work and to enter his imaginative world, a reader must put himself in the position of an actor and explore with an actor's practical and patient cunning.

All actors live with their parts and, to varying degrees, they live in and through them as well. This sets a level of engagement that is not easily imitated by a reader, however much he may wish to do so. But an Elizabethan actor had one great encouragement to personal identification which is almost unknown today, and this is something that can be reproduced very easily by a reader to provide a start in the right direction. The actor of Shakespeare's day was not given a copy of the play in which he was to perform, but only the words of his part and a few other words which provided the cues on which he must speak. If we write out a whole role in this way and study only those words for a few days, some sense of an actor's engagement may be gained and a measure of Shakespeare's constant attention to his needs and opportunities.

Here is the 'part' of the nameless Messenger in the opening scene of *Much Ado About Nothing*, with cues of four words in *italics*:

 . . .   *this night to Messina.*

He is very near by this; he was not three leagues off when I left him.

. . . lost in this action?
But few of any sort, and none of name.

. . . young Florentine called Claudio.
Much deserv'd on his part, and equally rememb'red by Don Pedro. He hath borne himself beyond the promise of his age, doing, in the figure of a lamb, the feats of a lion; he hath, indeed, better bett'red expectation than you must expect of me to tell you how.

. . . much glad of it.
I have already delivered him letters, and there appears much joy in him; even so much that joy could not show itself modest enough without a badge of bitterness.

. . . break out into tears?
In great measure.

. . . the wars or no?
I know none of that name, lady; there was none such in the army of any sort.

. . . Signior Benedick of Padua.
O, he's return'd, and as pleasant as ever he was.

. . . I doubt it not.
He hath done good service, lady, in these wars.

. . . hath an excellent stomach.
And a good soldier, too, lady.

. . . he to a lord?
A lord to a lord, a man to a man; stuff'd with all honourable virtues.

. . . a new sworn brother.
Is't possible?

. . . with the next block.
I see, lady, the gentleman is not in your books.

. . . him to the devil?
He is most in the company of the right noble Claudio.

. . . pound ere 'a be cured.
I will hold friends with you, lady.

. . . till a hot January.
Don Pedro is approach'd.

An actor receiving these words to study will know that the man he represents comes from a battlefield with news of Don Pedro, a victorious commander. He is among friends, but speaks at first as if he required two shots at every verbal target: 'he is . . . he was'; 'but few . . . and none'; 'much deserv'd . . . equally rememb'red' – and so on, with lengthening phrases and more figurative speech as he gains attention and confidence. A precise question about 'tears' leaves him for the first time with only one thing to say: 'In great measure.' Is it against his soldierly nature to speak directly about weeping? He had already referred to this subject, but metaphorically, using a military 'badge' to convey his true meaning. A second question restores his double-barrelled confidence:

> I know none of that name, lady; there was none such in the army of any sort.

Probably he is something of a show-off, because he is here implying his wide knowledge of the battle, as in his first speech he had intimated that he had personal contact with Don Pedro. Yet he is pleased to give happy news unofficially: 'O, he's return'd . . . '. Perhaps 'He hath done good service, lady, in these wars' – with 'lady' breaking the one reply into two – can be spoken as if he is direct and soldierly at first, and then remembers that his questioner should know little of what lies behind 'service' in a military context. But 'service' could be a flirtatious joke or slip of the tongue, which is then gallantly corrected. (Shakespeare and other writers of the time often played on the military and sexual meanings of 'service'; and, as we shall see, double-meanings are ricocheting all round the Messenger by this time in the scene.) In any case, he has been drawn now into conscious word-play with the lady, and his part is to insist on military meanings and values, until brought to a halt with 'Is't possible?'. This is the Messenger's first question, and an actor studying the part, will know that he has come now to a full-stop: he is no longer giving information and has lost confidence. The 'lady' has in some way got the better of him in cross-talk, and the actor will have to look for some new way of regaining initiative and re-establishing the audience's interest in his role.

The next three speeches provide the means for recovery. They are firm and, although twice pointed with 'lady', each makes its statement in one sustained phrase. Probably he stands more to attention now than at ease. Yet the ride is bumpy: his first rejoinder sounds like a polite signing-off and the second is a strictly factual response to a question which must have been outrageous enough to warrant the use of 'devil'. The actor who tries to make his mark as the Messenger will find the third of these short speeches the most useful: 'I will hold friends with you, lady'; in this he recognises his adversary's superior verbal power but pits his own personal dignity against it. However its success is limited: he may speak strongly, but that does not keep the fantastic at bay. His next cue is 'hot January', which means that talk is still combative and hard to manage.

But here he gets his last chance. He takes the lead away from other speakers with an absolute change of tone and a new subject for attention: 'Don Pedro is approach'd.' The Messenger may be interpreting an off-stage trumpet-call which everyone hears but only he can understand; or he may have detached himself from the cross-talk so decisively that he can pick up a distant sound of the commander's approach. Either way, the Messenger is at once very alert, knowledgeable and soldier-like. Nothing implies that he leaves the stage at this point, so it is not an exit-line. It is, simply, his last shot, and every actor will try to make a large and precise impression with these four formal words.

In this very small part, Shakespeare has offered the actor a clear individual development at the start of the scene, when everyone must listen to his news; and then an opportunity to suggest more than is spoken, followed by quicker interplay, a loss of confidence, a rally, a more personal statement and, then, a final flourish. By turns, the Messenger speaks with authority, off-the-cuff, uncertainly and, sometimes, at ease when he sustains the line of his own thoughts with buoyant rhythms. Although his main task is to provide information, the lines he has been given must be spoken so that he varies the nature of his engagement with the other characters on stage, suggesting different levels of consciousness and involvement. The give-and-take has energy, changing rhythms, changing diction, reversals and surprises. The last switch to an official announcement will be far more impressive in the dramatic context Shakespeare has prepared for it than the four simple words could indicate by themselves. Some gesture seems called for: standing to attention or saluting; or moving ostentatiously to a new position which will break the pattern established in previous talk, and will allow Don Pedro to up-stage everyone else. The final physical movement that the actor invents, just before the audience's attention is taken away from him, may be his most individual mark in the play; a lively impression of an earnest, young and politely self-conscious soldier.

Once the actor is on-stage for rehearsals, he will realise more fully what is required of him and what are his opportunities. He is in travelling dress showing the marks of battle and he is surrounded by three very attentive civilians, who are informally at ease in their own home and talk about their own secrets and make their own jokes. The 'lady' with whom he talks is Beatrice and she silences him early on by speaking about eating men who have been killed in battle. The Messenger returns to the conversation only after old Leonato has intervened. 'Is't possible?' is more of a defeat than appeared at first, for he has just been silent a second time after Beatrice has mocked his words and emptied them of meaning. This time Leonato has apologised: 'You must not, sir, mistake my niece . . .'. The affirmation of 'I will hold

friends with you, lady' will need to be that much stronger to stand up to
the energy of Beatrice's wit; but, however positively it is spoken, the
conflict still continues. Beatrice's more simple reply, 'Do, good friend',
maintains contact and echoes mockingly his tone of voice. The
Messenger's last short speech does not answer the lady, but cuts across
her talk with Leonato who has intervened to make light of her
aggressive spirit:

> LEON. You will never run mad, niece.
> BEAT. No, not till a hot January.

Perhaps the manner in which the Messenger announces Don Pedro's
approach expresses a sense of relief as he escapes from word-play and
courtesy to the normal business of military life. He will have to make his
words register over against Beatrice's wild and dancing fantasy which
has not allowed her to ask after Benedick except through an outrageous
nickname – and this her uncle either did not recognise or pretended not
to do so. For a moment, Shakespeare invites the Messenger to hold the
puzzling world of 'much ado about nothing' quite still and attentive, in
preparation for the entry of a conquerer. Now the actor of this small
part has every prospect of enjoying his performance.

The basic question underlying this examination of the words of one part
has been 'How does the actor act?' This may not be the first enquiry to
be made in preparation of a new role, and some others might probe
more deeply: 'What kind of man is this?' 'What does he look like?'
'What makes him say these words and not others?' 'How best can these
words be spoken?' Some would lead to unnecessary complications:
'What can I do with this line?' 'How can I make an audience listen?'
While all these approaches have their own rewards, the attempt to
imagine an actor's performance supporting the words of his part raises
specifically theatrical issues in a comparatively simple way so that they
can be understood by a reader. It will lead on to most other aspects of a
part including the larger ones involving relationships with other
performances and with the action of a whole play.

In my experience, questions about 'character' are the most difficult of
all in preparing a Shakespearean role. Unless he has a sudden
inspiration or is given a definitive lead by a director of the play, an actor
has no choice but to work blind in this respect. Like Gloucester in *Lear*
he 'smells his way to Dover'. He 'finds' the character while he is trying
to make his words work as part of a continuous act, and as the play
comes to life around him in rehearsal and performance. He is suspicious

of verbal definitions or descriptions of the role he plays, and prefers to trust his own work with the text and with the other actors. This means that if we are to respond to the plays as performers do, a reader or critic should delay any discussion of characters until he has undertaken a thorough enquiry about the actors' performances. In the first instance, we should ask what an actor must do, not what is the nature of the character he portrays.

Elizabethan plays had no 'characters' as we speak of them, and no reader or actor undertook character-analysis. 'Characterisation' was a word used by mathematicians.* In published dramatic texts of the early seventeenth century, a cast-list might be printed with the heading 'The Persons Represented', but more usual forms were 'The Principal Actors' or 'Actors Names'. The 'List of Characters' with which we are familiar today dates only from the mid-eighteenth century, and it is only a few years earlier that extended critical discussions of dramatic characters began to appear. The present-day theatrical usage derives from the way novelists wrote about their art, and not from the dramatists or the theatre. An Elizabethan actor was concerned with his 'part' and its performance, and so he 'presented' the appropriate 'person' for the living illusion of the play. If we think as he did and study a text in the same way, we shall be close to Shakespeare's own working concepts.

When we followed the Messenger's part, we did begin to recognise a particular person. I wrote of 'an earnest, young and politely self-conscious soldier', although no word of the text warrants any part of my portrayal. This description of him was one way of recording the dynamics of the scene as they relate to the role of the Messenger, especially in relation to Leonato and Beatrice. The definition emerged only after a discussion of what the actor must do to support the words of his part. However, the clearest impression of a 'person' in action was

---

* The nearest to a concept of dramatic character was that of a 'humour', as used by Ben Jonson – cf. Induction, *Every Man out of his Humour*:

> As when some one peculiar quality
> Doth so possess a man, that it doth draw
> All his affects, his spirits, and his powers,
> In their confluxions, all to run one way.

Shakespeare usually used 'humour' in the more general senses of a man's temperament, mood or whim; when he used it to define how a man acted, a note of mockery is usually unmistakable, as in *Henry V*, ii i 74 and ii iii 63.

By Restoration times, pithy definitions of each 'character' in a play were often provided by dramatists. This Theophrastian usage occurs sporadically in a few Jacobean plays, but belongs more properly to the wittily designed plots of the neo-classical Restoration theatre.

derived from considering the interplay of several independent performances, and these more elaborate issues should be the next claim on a reader's attention.

☆

As we have noted already, the main actors in Shakespeare's plays were sharers in their own acting company and so had particular occasion to study each other. But all actors, once they are on stage, are dependent on collaboration, mutual understanding and generous give-and-take. No matter how zealously an individual actor has studied his part, he has to act in full contact with his fellows if he wants to use his text appropriately and make a strong, individual contribution to the play in performance. Each scene has a corporate life, its own rhythms, its own shape, tone, weight, movement, its centres of interest, its conflicts, developments, crises, resolutions; and these can be assessed only as the product of all the performances functioning together. In rehearsal and performance a scene begins to 'come together' so that everyone involved recognises that it 'works'. Individual problems are resolved unobtrusively and the various parts begin to be defined more clearly.

A reader can take some steps towards this further understanding by asking how the 'lead' in dialogue is passed from one actor to another and by maintaining a comparative view wherever possible. Rosencrantz and Guildenstern offer a small-scale example. Common opinion believes that these parts in *Hamlet* are conveniences of the dramatist, filling out a scene, running messages, talking with the prince, serving as spies and couriers for Claudius. Critics write of them together as a pair of courtiers who are indistinguishable one from the other. But no actor could think this way if he played one of them, or if he had to act on stage with them. For a start, Rosencrantz says almost twice as much as Guildenstern and, although they customarily enter and leave the stage together, it is Rosencrantz, according to the Folio text, who enters on one occasion alone, ahead of Guildenstern (iv iii).

In their introductory scene with the King and Queen (ii ii), both are silent at first. Here are their two parts, with the cue-lines:

ROSENCRANTZ
As fits a king's remembrance.
                     Both your Majesties
Might, by the sovereign power you have of us,
Put your dread pleasures more into command
Than to entreaty.

GUILDENSTERN

Than to entreaty.
          But we both obey,
And here give up ourselves, in the full bent,
To lay our service freely at your feet,
To be commanded.

And bring these gentlemen where Hamlet is.
Heavens make our presence and our practices
Pleasant and helpful to him!

The two actors will have to speak with fluent and nicely pointed courtesy: they will chime together, very aware of each other's rhythms. But even the words of their parts, on closer examination, show a difference between them. While Rosencrantz is the first to speak, it is he who emphasises the *dread* power of the King and Queen. Guildenstern's opening is more blunt – 'But we both obey' – and when he conforms to his partner's longer rhythms he uses the image of a bow *bent* to kill.

Once in rehearsal the two young men are revealed as opposites or even rivals. Guildenstern's first speech ends on a half-line which proves to be the only incomplete verse-line in the episode – and, therefore, the only pause dictated by Shakespeare's text. If he is to make this break in the dialogue work, the actor must speak with firm and confident emphasis, closing strongly as he picks up *command* from his fellow's previous speech. In view of this, we may wonder whether Guildenstern's first words interrupt the less decisive Rosencrantz, rather than follow where he had finished. Before leaving the stage, Guildenstern takes time to add a formal expression of good wishes, and is cunning enough to use the word 'practices'. This could mean, simply, 'what we undertake'; but in the context, the alternative – and, in Shakespeare, more usual – sense of 'stratagems, tricks, deceits' may also register. (This usage is very clear elsewhere in *Hamlet*, notably at iv vii 67 and 138.) So, while Rosencrantz has nothing to say when they are sent away on their business, Guildenstern acknowledges, lightly and ambiguously, that he goes to spy on his friend, the Prince: a fact that all the other speeches have glossed over. He has touched the most delicate issue. Perhaps his words, if not his initiative, cause Rosencrantz to stop in the middle of an elaborate bow to the King or to turn back from a speedy exit to listen. Possibly, Rosencrantz does not notice what his partner has said and done; this might be due to thoughtlessness or to a more devious and self-protecting cunning. In whatever way Guildenstern's speech and Rosencrantz's silence are played, a difference between the two young men will clearly register as they hold attention by the action of leaving the stage.

Their last moment on stage is prolonged further by a reply. The King does not speak, but the Queen does. The simplicity and directness of her 'Aye amen!' is unprecedented in this episode. This could be the only fervent speech to break a cool, elaborate and polite surface in the interview: a brief recognition that all the talk has been about a prince's dangerous madness and his pitiable grief. Do the two young men respond, halting their exit once more? Does the King respond? The next words suggest that Polonius is the first to break the mood with purposeful abruptness:

> Th'ambassadors from Norway, my good Lord,
> Are joyfully return'd.

Of course, the Queen might have said 'Aye amen!' thoughtlessly, eager to hurry the young men off stage as her previous speech suggests. In this case Rosencrantz's silence will be more in tune with court behaviour and double-talk: he might smile as he leaves, while Guildenstern is more watchful. The smoothness of Rosencrantz and the cutting mind of Guildenstern are not fully apparent in the words of their parts, but gain prominence as the scene comes alive through all four performances. Postures, actions and manner of speech accentuate the differences of their words. Eyes move quickly during the talk and bodies may be alert and nervous, in contrast to the more sustained rhythms of some speeches. Both young men are restricted in physical movement, especially while the king opens with a non-stop address of 18 lines. Rosencrantz is the discreet courtier; Guildenstern more the soldier; either could be a dangerous operator.

Such a comparison must be speculative. Shakespeare's text allows great variety of exploration and, as soon as the play is set in action, the text offers issues for intuitive choice. As we read attentively we need to imagine an active and personal reality which can support the words at every point. Each small particular of that reality has to be believable as part of a human act; each part or role must make continuous sense; and the whole consort of parts has to gain credence in lively interplay. The text on the printed page is our one guide and the one touchstone by which everything must be assessed, but we have to travel, imaginatively, far beyond it, filling out the play until it is a lively image of life. The words of each part have to be given a body, that can be seen and felt; and each of these created persons must be endowed with consistent and continuous energy.

Some method can support this adventure. We should watch,

consciously, for exchanges of 'lead' in the talk, and question the motives for them. Unexpected interruptions and withdrawals into silence should be especially marked. Sometimes a speech is notable for what it does not say or for the way double meanings are suggested or refused. We should ask where each person on stage is looking at each moment; eye-contact or a momentary shift of attention alters the effect of what is said. We should know, at every moment, what each person is doing; if no physical movement is required, then we should note how everyone is standing, what their postures express. Individual entries and exits always draw the audience's eye, and an actor uses them to start and finish a scene with a distinct impression, whether he has words to say or not. Gestures and pauses that are described or implied by the text must be considered as carefully as the speeches; but as words depend on acts, so actions must never be divorced from words or assessed as self-contained dramatic statements. Always a complete human reality must be imagined, in all its complicated means of expression and complicated interactions.

A short episode offers the most immediate pleasures of recreation, because our fantasy lives most easily in moments. But a play is more than a collection of fragments. Each part calls for continuous performance, consistent both psychologically and physically. In a theatre, the actor's sense of his performance, its rhythms, development, moments of strength and revelation, will shape each new discovery of what he can do with his part into a convincing and playable whole. The plain fact that a single actor carries out each part means that in performance every part will have some basic coherence and continuity according to that actor's individual potential, but this is harder to achieve in a reader's mind. Special watch must be kept on continuity, and the best recourse is to study in isolation, once again, the text of each actor's part, enquiring now about what are its constant features and how new elements can be introduced, established and developed.

Rosencrantz and Guildenstern return a second time in Act II scene ii, and encounter Hamlet. Here is Guildenstern's part, again with the cue-lines:

> *God save you, sir!*
> My honour'd lord!
>
> *. . . indifferent children of the earth.*
> Happy in that we are not over-happy;
> On fortune's cap we are not the very button.

> . . . *or in the middle of her favours?*
>> Faith, her privates we.

> . . . *she sends you to prison hither?*
>> Prison, my lord!

> . . . *were it not that I have bad dreams.*
>> Which dreams indeed are ambition; for the very substance
>> of the ambitious is merely the shadow of a dream.

> . . . *for, by my fay, I cannot reason.*
>> We'll wait upon you.   [*spoken with Rosencrantz*]

> . . . *Come, come; nay, speak.*
>> What should we say, my lord?

> . . . *If you love me, hold not off.*
>> My lord, we were sent for.

> *Is't possible?*
>> O, there has been much throwing about of brains.

> . . . *if philosophy could find it out.*   [*a flourish, off-stage*]
>> There are the players.

> . . . *my uncle-father and aunt-mother are deceived.*
>> In what, my dear lord?

Only twice does Guildenstern speak with a courtier's fluency, and then
his rhythms are shorter than before. In his second lengthy reply, in
prose, he seems to repeat himself, as if his invention flags. The
remarkable features of the part in this episode are how briefly he speaks
and how frequently this is in response to a direct enquiry. After the first
two speeches, where he half-echoes Rosencrantz, all the others follow a
cue from Hamlet. He asks two questions: the first queries his own
response; but the second interrogates Hamlet, with the more familiar
'my dear lord' pressing on his attention. Although Guildenstern is on
stage in this scene for another 130 lines, he has nothing more to say: he
will watch and respond to the developing drama – and a very great deal
is happening – without betraying his thoughts in the clarity or duplicity
of words. His mind is active still, as his looks will reveal. After he has
confessed to serving the king – and here Rosencrantz is silent and
evasive – Guildenstern's next speech, alluding to the Tragedians of the
City, is an airy acknowledgement that 'there has been much throwing
about of brains': his own brain is now more narrowly and consistently
involved. Guildenstern says little and yet is highly alert; and he is the
one who faces Hamlet squarely.

Later in the play Guildenstern becomes still more reserved, verbally.
But he does not weaken: it is he who bears the King's message after the
play-scene in III ii, and he brings Hamlet on stage under guard in IV iii.

The Prince seems to acknowledge Guildenstern's superior strength by singling him out for an ironic attack, introduced with talk of hunting:

> To withdraw with you – why do you go about to recover the wind of me, as if you would drive me into a toil?
> GUILD. O my lord, if my duty be too bold, my love is too unmannerly.
> HAMLET. I do not well understand that. Will you play upon this pipe?
> GUILD. My lord, I cannot.
> HAMLET. I pray you.
> GUILD. Believe me, I cannot.
> HAMLET. I do beseech you.
> GUILD. I know no touch of it, my lord.
> HAMLET. It is as easy as lying: govern these ventages with your fingers and thumb, give it breath with your mouth, and it will discourse most eloquent music. Look you, these are the stops.
> GUILD. But these cannot I command to any utterance of harmony; I have not the skill.
> HAMLET. Why, look you now, how unworthy a thing you make of me! You would play upon me; you would seem to know my stops; you would pluck out the heart of my mystery; you would sound me from my lowest note to the top of my compass. . . . (III ii 337 ff.)

Guildenstern says nothing more in reply and we see him next with the King, where he takes the initiative away from Rosencrantz in another short sentence: 'We will ourselves provide' (III iii 7). An actor will keep the quiet force of Guildenstern's later appearances as a surprise for the audience: a new development that makes its effect as he gains confidence in his part and as the play's narrative involves him in more violent and unambiguous action. But in choosing how to play his earliest appearances, with their fluent speeches, he must prefer those possibilities which will render his later transformation more credible and give the conviction of inward continuity to the varying aspects of his impersonation.

Some scholars have argued that the formal qualities of Elizabethan dramatic speech, especially its rhetorical and metrical structures, are so different from the freedom of ordinary speech that the actors of those days would have been unable to imitate life on the stage. It is suggested that so much of their attention must have been given to techniques of elocution and to niceties of meaning and form that we should consider them more as orators than as actors in the modern sense. Although books of rhetoric, by classical, European and English authors, have been quoted in support of this notion, all the *theatrical* evidence is against it. Richard Flecknoe's *Short Discourse of the English Stage*, published in

1664, presented the issue clearly. Richard Burbage, chief actor of the Chamberlain's Men and the first performer of many of the major Shakespearean roles, is there credited with 'all the parts of an excellent orator, animating his words with speaking, and speech with action'; but Flecknoe then adds significantly:

> . . . yet even then, he was an excellent actor still, never falling from his part when he had done speaking; but with his looks and gesture, maintaining it still unto the height.

Burbage had the clarity and eloquence of an orator, respecting the artifice of the text, but he also lived imaginatively in performance:

> . . . he was a delightful Proteus, so wholly transforming himself into his part, and putting off himself with his clothes, as he never (not so much as in the tyring-house) assum'd himself again until the play was done.[1]

Shakespeare has Hamlet speak in much the same terms. In his view, an actor holds 'the mirror up to nature' and 'imitates' humanity (III ii 16, 34). It is Hamlet, the amateur actor, who is praised only for speaking 'with good accent and good discretion' (II ii 460–1); it is the leading professional who

> . . . in a fiction, in a dream of passion,
> Could force his soul so to his own conceit
> That from her working all his visage wann'd;
> Tears in his eyes, distraction in's aspect,
> A broken voice, and his whole function suiting
> With form to his conceit. . .   (II ii 545–50)

The First Player, in his recitation of the Pyrrhus speech and without the build-up of the rest of the drama from which it was taken, 'turn'd his colour' and had 'tears in's eyes' (II ii 513–14).

Although the actors of Shakespeare's day did indeed speak with precision, so that single words could register strongly (as with 'mobled queen' in the First Player's recitation) and so that the harmonies of the verse had full effect, they also gave their audiences the illusion of life being lived. Recurrent phrases in accounts of acting are 'lively', 'likeness of truth', 'to the life', 'perfect imitation', 'true imitation of life', 'naturally'. We are told that what we see the actor 'personate' we think 'truly done before us'. It was said that members of an audience had rushed on to the stage to save a hero from a threatened blow, and that, for a joke, a young male actor had masqueraded successfully off-stage as a citizen's wife.

George Chapman prided himself on being a literary man, but he wrote his plays for performance:

Scenical representation is so far from giving just cause of any least diminution, that the personal and exact life it gives to any history or other such delineation of human actions, adds to them lustre, spirit, and apprehension. (Dedication, *Caesar and Pompey*)

For Thomas Heywood, a dramatist a few years younger than either Shakespeare or Chapman, the actor's *action*, and not his speech, provided the magic of performance, its power to 'bewitch'.

So bewitching a thing is lively and spirited action that it hath power to new mould the hearts of the spectators and fashion them to the shape of any noble and notable attempt.

If a soldier was called for in a play, then the audience must actually 'see a soldier, shaped like a soldier, walk, speak, act like a soldier'.[2]

Lording Barry, another younger dramatist, promised in the Prologue to *Ram Alley* (1611) that the actors would

> . . .   show
> Things never done, with that true life
> That thoughts and wits shall stand at strife,
> Whether the things now shown be true,
> Or whether we ourselves now do
> The things we but present.

When a dramatist called upon performers to go beyond ordinary experience, they had to ensure that the audience believed everything to be true to life and actually happening.

Undoubtedly Elizabethan acting was different from any we know today and we might not recognise its 'perfect imitation'. (In the same way, Giotto's paintings were considered amazingly lifelike in his own time and are often valued today for other qualities.) If a time-machine were to transport us to Shakespeare's Globe, the odds are that we would find the performances strong, bold, stark, very active, simply delineated and clearly enunciated. The actor's attention to metre and syntactical structure might appear excessively marked at first hearing, but we would soon learn to appreciate the subtle naturalism that was contained and defined by this basic formality. We would also come to realise that for Shakespeare's audience there was less difference than we thought at first between stage life and real life: the manners of that time were much more formal than our own, intimacy more rare in everyday life, and public speech more carefully deliberate. For the well-off and well-born – and that is for most of the people represented in plays – clothes were stiffer and more elaborately decorated; this was especially so for women, hence a young male actor could readily hide his own figure.

The audience around us at the Globe would give a spirited response to the show, appreciating a 'personal and exact' imitation of life itself. Artifice and virtuosity thrived on the Elizabethan stage, without inhibiting the actors' re-creation of life. Roars of applause and hand-clapping accompanied the progress of a play, as the audience entered imaginatively into the life of the drama, appreciating its excitements and its skill. In the anonymous *Tragedy of Sir John van Olden Barnavelt*, the hero is likened to a leading player:

> . . . with such murmurs as glad spectators in a theatre grace their best actors with, they ever heard him, when to have had a sight of him was held a prosperous omen; when no eye gazed on him that was not filled with admiration.   (lines 2475–82)

As early as 1592, Thomas Nashe wrote that 'Talbot, terror of the French', had been honoured in theatres by 'the tears of ten thousand spectators at least' – and this because 'in the tragedian that represents his person' they 'imagine they behold him fresh bleeding'.[3] We are so accustomed to sitting discreetly in darkened auditoriums that the active participation of Elizabethan audiences would be quite as amazing to us as any difference in acting styles. Theatre-going was more like going to a football match, and the actors responded to encouragement: the build-up of emotional climaxes in the drama was punctuated and sustained by vocal applause, and suspense was stretched and tested in an almost breathless silence.

The repertoire of Elizabethan theatres was so busy that very few plays were performed more frequently than once a week; during the long season in London an active company would often give six different performances during a working week of six afternoons. This allowed little time for rehearsals. About thirty different plays would be staged within six months, and about half of these would be first performances. An actor's most careful study must have been in private, as he examined and memorised his part. Most of the company's rehearsal time would be needed to ensure that entries and exits were in good order, and fights and other complicated stage-business properly and safely managed as required by the text. When an audience watched the play come to life, the actors were encountering each other's performances, realising afresh the opportunities of the text and responding to the audience's encouragement, all at the same time. A play in performance was an unrepeatable occasion, providing a new life for the text on that particular afternoon, with new emphases and interpretations. It was an improvised engagement, depending on skill, individual preparation and collaborative experience. Only practice could give actors confidence, and only strong imagination could allow them to respond to whatever concerns were in the air, for performers and audience alike. The actor had to win the day afresh, at each performance: this, above all, ensured that the audience followed the action closely, willing it to be true.

To a good memory, a clear sense of his part, a practised ear and eye for opportunities as they occurred, a lively imagination and a strong personal confidence, the Elizabethan actor had to add great physical energy. He had to sustain his performance without carefully placed rests and without thorough drilling of complicated stage-business. He was always on the move: the stage was forty feet wide and thirty deep, and the audience had to be faced, and pleased, on at least three sides. Impersonations and reactions had to be so complete physically that the changing dramatic situation was expressed from all points of view. The stage was not a picture, looked at from one direction, like most of ours, but an arena or boxing-ring. Figures in action caught the eye, and held it by changing from moment to moment.

Very little attempt was made to 'dress' the stage with the accoutrements of ordinary life; at the most, a table, chairs, a throne, a tomb, an arbour would be introduced to focus and to add meaning and variety to the action. The busy 'traffic of the stage' allowed no time to prepare all the particulars that could give an appearance of a lived-in room as appropriate to any one individual person at any particular time; no one even thought about this kind of naturalism to which we are accustomed by some current theatre practice and nearly all films and television dramas. The lifelikeness of any play was presented by corporate and expressive *action*, the persons of the play encountering each other as responsive and dynamic beings. When an English company toured Germany, the people, not 'understanding a word they said, both men and women, flocked wonderfully to see their gesture and action'.[4]

The wealth of words in one of Shakespeare's plays can be appreciated at first glance at the text, but we have only to set the persons in action in our minds, on something like the open stage of the Globe theatre, to understand that its physical realisation has a comparable richness and makes demands upon the actors that are equally great. There are fights, chases, dances, fits of madness, many changes of costume, swift and large alterations of location and mood, seemingly endless shifts of intention, posture, gesture and movement. Two groups of persons have contrasting actions; a solitary figure moves around and between the others; a formal group is suddenly disturbed or splits into rival factions; travellers arrive in haste or weariness; pageants or symbolic objects are revealed suddenly, and plays are enacted within the on-going drama while their on-stage audiences have their own vocal and physical life. And throughout all this varied activity, the rhythms of speech call for highly dynamic utterance, which cannot be given without quick physical resource, varied emotional pitch and lively intelligence. Often the cues come quickly one after another, a new speech cutting off or surpassing its predecessor. Sometimes the actor has to speak 30 or more lines of verse, altering intention, pace, rhythm, pitch and volume as his mind races and hesitates; and at the same time, his body must respond to the changing drama, and so provide the centre of visual focus on the large stage and sustain the truth and complexity of his performance.

The danger for an Elizabethan actor was obvious: he might strut and bellow to keep attention at any price, and strive to out-Herod Herod. But mere force would do violence to the play and his own resources. He needed to exercise consummate control in order to achieve that variety of physical and mental excitement which could match the playwright's quick-moving fantasy through two and a half or three hours of performance. He needed to be mettlesome, as are almost all of Shakespeare's writings: alert, quick-witted, deeply sensitive, physically responsive, unashamedly and easily skilful, imaginative and totally committed; his intelligence had to be active, expressive and generously reciprocal.

We must imagine the plays with their various persons in full action and interaction. They may then provide a living image of life, defined by words and sustained, explored and illuminated by action.

5 | *Plays for Actors*

When a reader tries to enter a play by Shakespeare as if he were an actor, he must respond in his imagination with his whole being. He must seek an 'act' that, with Shakespeare's words, will 'give life' to the text.

Sometimes this is an obvious demand. In early works, descriptions of action that should accompany words show that the physical element of performance was sometimes at fever pitch. For example, the Duke of Suffolk in *Henry VI, Part Two* speaks of cursing his enemies:

> I would invent as bitter searching terms,
> As curst, as harsh, and horrible to hear,
> Deliver'd strongly through my fixed teeth,
> With full as many signs of deadly hate,
> As lean-fac'd Envy in her loathsome cave.
> My tongue should stumble in mine earnest words,
> Mine eyes should sparkle like the beaten flint,
> Mine hair be fix'd on end, as one distract;
> Ay, every joint should seem to curse and ban;   . . . (III ii 311–19)

The whole body, besides face and voice, expresses meaning; and even as he is describing all this, the actor must show a heart ready to break:

> And even now my burden'd heart would break,
> Should I not curse them.   (320–21)

As Suffolk pictures a stumbling, tortured and blazing enactment of hatred, he speaks as if he is about to die, his heart failing.

Richard, Duke of Gloucester, and later King Richard the Third, is very aware of physical engagement. He can 'snarl, and bite, and play the dog' (*3 Henry VI*, v vi 77). More dangerously, he knows,

> Why, I can smile, and murder whiles I smile,
> And cry 'Content!' to that which grieves my heart,
> And wet my cheeks with artificial tears,
> And frame my face to all occasions.   . . . (*3 H.VI*, III ii 182–5)

49

With the Duke of Buckingham, in Act III of *Richard III*, he gives a performance that is alive in every vein, nerve, sinew and breath:

> GLOU.   Come, cousin, canst thou quake and change thy colour,
> Murder thy breath in middle of a word,
> And then again begin, and stop again,
> As if thou wert distraught and mad with terror?
> BUCK.   Tut, I can counterfeit the deep tragedian;
> Speak and look back, and pry on every side,
> Tremble and start at wagging of a straw,
> Intending deep suspicion. Ghastly looks
> Are at my service, like enforced smiles;
> And both are ready in their offices
> At any time to grace my stratagems.   . . .   (*R. III*, III v 1–11)

Here the two dukes must speak lightly of the 'deep' performance of tragedians, but other tensions must underly their own performances if the next words – brief, taut and questioning – are to be 'truly' enacted:

> But what, is Catesby gone?
> GLOU.   He is; and, see, he brings the mayor along.
> BUCK.   Lord Mayor . . .

And then the fun begins – a buoyant representation of alarm.

In later plays Shakespeare wrote with less elation about 'ghastly' actions, but demanded the same pitch of performance. So Gertrude describes her son on the last appearance in *Hamlet* of the Ghost:

> Forth at your eyes your spirits wildly peep;
> And, as the sleeping soldiers in th'alarm,
> Your bedded hairs like life in excrements
> Start up and stand on end. O gentle son,
> Upon the heat and flame of thy distemper
> Sprinkle cool patience.   . . .   (III iv 119–24)

When Macbeth meets the Witches for the first time, Banquo is at hand to mark his silent response:

> Good sir, why do you start, and seem to fear
> Things that do sound so fair?   . . .   (I iii 51–2)

At the ceremonial banquet, after Banquo's Ghost has appeared, Lady Macbeth remonstrates:

> O, these flaws and starts –
> Imposters to true fear – would well become
> A woman's story at a winter's fire,
> Authoriz'd by her grandam. Shame itself!
> Why do you make such faces?   . . .   (III iv 63–7)

When the Ghost reappears, Macbeth himself knows that he is reduced to 'trembling' like a frightened child and that his face is strangely 'blanch'd' (III v 103–6, 112–16).

Such violent crises cannot exist alone. Throughout the plays, if we are to read them in the way Shakespeare imagined them, each speech must be conceived as part of an act which involves the whole body of the actor. A scene in *Twelfth Night* contains these words:

> 'Tis but fortune; all is fortune. Maria once told me she did affect me; and I have heard herself come thus near, that, should she fancy, it should be one of my complexion. Besides, she uses me with a more exalted respect than any one else that follows her. What should I think on't? . . . To be Count Malvolio! . . . There is example for't: the Lady of the Strachy married the yeoman of the wardrobe. . . . Having been three months married to her, sitting in my state . . .   (II v 22–41)

So Malvolio day-dreams about his future, but these words are not all. Fabian is present to tell us that the steward's whole being is inflated and that he struts and preens with self-obsessed fantasy:

> . . . Contemplation makes a rare turkey cock of him; how he jets under his advanced plumes!
> . . . Now he's deeply in: look how imagination blows him.   (28–9, 39–40)

Despite frequent silences, Malvolio gives a sustained performance: Fabian's word 'deeply' indicates that he has the intensity and completeness of a 'deep tragedian'. In Act III scene iv, Malvolio returns like a man 'possessed' and 'does nothing but smile'. This makes a huge impression, although he is silent at first, carried away by happiness. When he does speak, 'Sweet lady, ho ho' are all the words needed and all he has wit to summon. His physical performance says most: perhaps he trips over his own feet – his cross-gartering makes 'some obstruction in the blood' – or he may tremble and stutter as if inwardly afraid; or he may work hard, smiling and ogling; or he could relapse into giggling. We are told that he is soon kissing his hand again and again, and becomes outright 'bold'. Then he delivers a prepared speech, not hearing any of the interjections which attempt to stop him. Only a totally committed physical performance could sustain this absurd ecstasy.

Once we begin to imagine whole performances, we find that Shakespeare has provided many more cues for the actors than at first appeared. Here, for example, is a short, quiet scene from *Romeo and Juliet*:

Enter FRIAR LAWRENCE *and* ROMEO

F. L.   So smile the heavens upon this holy act
        That after-hours with sorrow chide us not!
ROM.   Amen, amen! But come what sorrow can,
        It cannot countervail the exchange of joy
        That one short minute gives me in her sight.
        Do thou but close our hands with holy words,
        Then love-devouring death do what he dare;
        It is enough I may but call her mine.
F. L.   These violent delights have violent ends,
        And in their triumph die; like fire and powder,
        Which, as they kiss, consume. The sweetest honey
        Is loathsome in his own deliciousness,
        And in the taste confounds the appetite.
        Therefore love moderately: long love doth so;
        Too swift arrives as tardy as too slow.

Enter JULIET

F. L.   Here comes the lady. O, so light a foot
        Will ne'er wear out the everlasting flint.
        A lover may bestride the gossamer
        That idles in the wanton summer air
        And yet not fall, so light is vanity.
JUL.   Good even to my ghostly confessor.
F. L.   Romeo shall thank thee, daughter, for us both.
JUL.   As much to him, else is his thanks too much.
ROM.   Ah, Juliet, if the measure of thy joy
        Be heap'd like mine, and that thy skill be more
        To blazon it, then sweeten with thy breath
        This neighbour air, and let rich music's tongue
        Unfold the imagin'd happiness that both
        Receive in either by this dear encounter.
JUL.   Conceit, more rich in matter than in words,
        Brags of his substance, not of ornament.
        They are but beggars than can count their worth;
        But my true love is grown to such excess
        I cannot sum up sum of half my wealth.
F. L.   Come, come with me, and we will make short work;
        For, by your leaves, you shall not stay alone
        Till holy church incorporate two in one.

Exeunt   (II vi)

The most direct instruction to an actor is the Friar's exclamation as
Juliet enters 'light' of foot; she must float, as it were, without disturbing
the least 'gossamer' that might be held aloft on a summer afternoon. But
this is only one ingredient in the physical reality of the scene. Speech

itself is a physical activity, involving expenditure of energy, change of breathing, heightened tension, nervous relaxation, sustained and broken rhythms. Words may also imply that a speaker changes the direction in which he faces, or becomes more intimate or distant. Once we listen to what the text tells us about physical activity, we shall find innumerable cues to what happens on the stage.

Although the Friar's speeches have sustained rhythms, they are strongly pointed. In the first two lines, the opposition between 'smile' and 'sorrow' prepares for the sharper juxtaposition of 'violent delights'; this is followed quickly by 'delights' and 'ends', 'triumph' and 'dies', 'kiss' and 'consume', 'sweetest' and 'loathsome', 'swift' and 'slow', and so on. The Friar must hold his ground, sharp-eyed, unsurprised, assured, firm and precise. In contrast, Romeo, starts with the impulsive repetition of 'Amen, amen!' and the springing avowal of 'But come what sorrow can'. His mind rushes from the delicacy of 'close our hands with holy words' to the harshness of 'love-devouring death do what he dare', which has the eager, simple impetus of alliteration. Then comes the unforced yet shattering simplicity of 'It is enough I may but call her mine', which means, literally, that he is prepared to die the moment after the marriage ceremony. He is a young man whose mind blazes, fire-like. He must be quick to look, move and speak, and to conclude whatever his imagination grasps. He can barely stand still beside the Friar.

It is then that Juliet enters. Romeo says nothing and neither does she. How do they meet? The answer to this, for one pair of actors, is given in a stage-direction of the 'Bad' Quarto version of the play, published in 1597: '*Enter* Juliet *somewhat fast, and embraceth* Romeo.' Almost certainly this is an eye-witness report of an early performance, and it shows that, on one occasion, the physical energies released by Juliet's arrival were quickly contained in the intimacy of an embrace. But, however it is acted, the moment they see each other must be alight with excitement and helpless bliss. They are silent then, and the Friar will be standing aside as he speaks his thoughts. His words are both tender and apprehensive. The change in tone, speed and rhythm from those of the brisk moralising of his earlier speech is marked. No longer does he clinch what he has to say with a couplet. This change in involvement must alter his physical bearing and bring a moment when dramatic action seems to stand still, with the lovers motionless in their embrace. Even if Juliet does not run to Romeo immediately, the two must stand still and silent as the Friar speaks, held together in the mutual 'joy' of meeting.

Juliet is the first to speak, but not to Romeo. She looks away from her husband-to-be and addresses the Friar with consciously simple politeness. The Friar's words may well be accompanied by a laugh at the absolute content that the lovers find in each other. She turns back to

Romeo and, a moment later, he finds his voice to express to her the fullness of his heart and mind. Leaping images and sustained rhythms leave him waiting for Juliet to speak; and she then replies, riding high and secure on an overflowing sense of arousal and possession. They may stand a little apart now, gazing into each other's eyes in sheer wonder, as their 'imagin'd happiness' unfolds to the 'neighbour air'. They are oblivious of everything else.

The Friar no longer debates what he or the lovers should do. The speed he counsels and the decisiveness with which he acts can have a comic effect. He had previously advised moderation and so now he may seem to jump to an emergency, suddenly afraid of leaving the two alone. But his change of tactics can also be affecting, as he recognises the strength of their feelings.

Romeo and Juliet have nothing more to say; but they leave side by side, under the Friar's guidance, to the wedding ceremony. They move with a new solemnity and, probably, as if in a dream. The Friar has to wait for them to go ahead – he cannot leave them alone – and so the audience's attention is focussed on the two silent lovers, on their mutual and expressive action as they move off-stage in whatever way seems 'lifelike' and 'true' to the actors who are realising their parts totally.

When we explore the stage-life of one of Shakespeare's plays, noting the innumerable cues to physical performance that are given by the words as they are spoken, we shall find that the relationship between the figures on the arena stage can be as eloquent as individual performances. The play is like a dance in which no performer is alone. Even when no one else is on-stage, the actor relates to the audience, and he often peoples the space around himself with imaginary persons and objects.

There are many ways in which we can become more aware of this interplay and engagement. The most obvious is clumsy and sometimes rather absurd; and it is more easily said than done. The trick is to take some upright objects, one to represent each person in a scene – a matchbox, pencil sharpener or bottle of glue, whatever is available on a desk or table – and then name them and fix a small label on each to represent a face. These crude dolls or manikins are then set up and made to meet each other as the text requires. The words that each person speaks should be spoken aloud as the reader's finger touches or moves the appropriate manikin. This is the simplest of model theatres and serves to keep a reader aware at all times of how the stage looks and how the persons of the play react to each other.

Such an experiment is not as easy as it sounds, but the difficulties that arise do lead to pertinent questions about the stage-life of a play.* The scene from Romeo and Juliet that we have just examined could be explored again in this way, and then another scene that should be just as simple. If the trick works then, a more ambitious exploration can be attempted. Complicated scenes may be chosen and the manikins developed. Chessmen or toy solders are a great improvement on random objects, especially when they are painted appropriate colours for each person in the play. These 'costumes' can be changed and hand-properties provided as the text suggests. The figures can be moved by more than one manipulator and each have its own reader. But in order to keep the object of the experiment clear, the text should always be read simply; full dramatisation of the words will confuse the issues that can be tackled with this toy theatre.

But manikins, however sophisticated, are poor substitutes for actors and suggest little more than the eloquence of groupings and regroupings, movements across the stage, variations of *tempi* and variations of engagement. The activity within each person on stage cannot be represented in this way, and so the experiment will hardly work at all for some scenes.

Another means of studying a play is to split the text into 'parts' once more and then follow each one separately, asking purely physical questions. How does this person stand? Is his weight equally on each foot or not? Is he at attention or at ease? Is his head up or down? And so on: how does he sit, or move? how quickly does he breath? where does he look? what are his hands doing? Many questions will have no answer, and the replies that do emerge may be very hesitant. But the routine is worth trying because it searches the text for actions that might accompany and sustain it.

Above all, a reader should try to acquire a sense of physical expressiveness. At any moment, the body of a human being makes a statement, even if this is, for the most part, unconscious. Usually there are three elements in this physical self-expression: a basic and continuous posture or state of being; a purposive activity; and an unconscious reaction or accompaniment to that purposive action. Very few human actions are simple, very few gestures are pure. Physical action is sometimes very subtle, and so the necessary first step towards understanding is to realise the great range of possible expression.

A book which teaches the elements of this language is Rudolf Laban's *The Mastery of Movement on the Stage* which is best read in Lisa Ullman's

---

* I often find that students who resist this 'play' as too fiddling or simple are those who become most addicted to the model stage as a three-dimensional form of study. (See also pp. 130–1, below.)

revised edition (1960).* Here movement is analysed in terms of Weight, Space, Time and Flow; and to show how these could combine in different ways, Laban devised a very simple exercise (p. 100). A reader of this book should stop now and make the following actions with hand and arm as boldly as possible:

> Pressing Action — firm, sustained, direct.
> Flicking Action — gentle, sudden, flexible.
> Wringing Action — firm, sustained, flexible.
> Dabbing Action — gentle, sudden, direct.
> Punching Action — firm, sudden, direct.
> Floating Action — gentle, sustained, flexible.
> Slashing Action — firm, sudden, flexible.
> Gliding Action — gentle, sustained, direct.

Once these various movements have been isolated, the reader should repeat each in turn and at the same time say aloud 'No' or 'Yes', allowing his speech to suit the action. Each single monosyllable will suggest distinctive meanings with each of the movements and so help to define the range of meanings implicit in the gestures.

Such an experiment only touches on the vast subject of physical expression and its relation to verbal language. Laban's book can take a reader much further, but a great deal of practical work is necessary before the action of actors – or of anyone else – can be read with subtlety and confidence. Fortunately, for the purposes of appreciating Shakespeare's plays and seeking out their full stage-life, a basic awareness of what movement and gesture can say gives immediate rewards. The text of a play is so full of suggestion that the seed of understanding will grow quickly. Shakespeare must have had a quick bodily sense and a fine eye; words came fittingly to mind as his imagination fed on what he had felt and seen.

If a reader can exercise some of an actor's patient, experimental search for appropriate gesture, movement and engagement, he will be better able to imagine the plays in action and performance.

Shakespeare's comedies, especially those set in pastoral countryside, give freest scope for physical exploration. (Perhaps these encounters were written in quicksilver manner so that the audience's attention was not left free to question the underlying sexual realities as the young men

* Here, and subsequently, when a book is recommended for study, the reader will find fuller details in 'Suggestions for Further Reading', p. 161, below.

took the female roles.) The lovers meet as wit and longings please, and a moment's surrender reverses what years had settled or introduces wholly new possibilities. If we follow Orlando and Rosalind in *As You Like It* as they come together in the Forest of Arden (Act III, scene ii), we may sense the lively dynamics of this imagined world.

Orlando says 'adieu' to Jaques, the 'good Monsieur Melancholy', and stands idly, lost in his own thoughts. Rosalind has been eavesdropping, accompanied by Celia, and now, after a quick word spoken aside, she walks boldly over to him: 'I will speak to him like a saucy lackey, and under that habit play the knave with him. – Do you hear, forester?' The very rhythm of Rosalind's last four words suggest a playful, punch-like encounter. He answers, 'Very well', and with this slashing reply he will turn suddenly – firmly and yet flexibly – aside. She stands 'like a saucy lackey' in man's clothes and goes by the name of Ganymede.

But what does she now do? Is there a pause while Orlando takes in the familiar face in a strange figure? His next words suggest a flicking movement, more gentle than his first: 'what would you?' He might look at her very briefly, genuinely puzzled. Rosalind's next words are less saucy, but sudden and unexpected (perhaps they pretend to casualness, dropping all pressure; she might move away a little): 'I pray you, what is't o'clock?' She has quite forgotten where she is and chooses a question at random. Orlando may break off the engagement, but probably just relaxes and laughs at the incongruity: 'You should ask me what time o'day; there's no clock in the forest.' Fearful of losing his attention, or impatient at her own mistake, Rosalind plays a stronger hand, almost leading with the word *lover* as a bait or test:

Then there is no true lover in the forest, else sighing every minute and groaning every hour would detect the lazy foot of Time as well as a clock.

Has Orlando been sighing and groaning after Jaques had bidden farewell to 'good Signior Love'? If so, Rosalind has probably had confidence to move closer to him; if not, she may be thinking of herself and so move away to finish at some distance from him. But there is no ambiguity about Orlando's reply, with its double question; he by-passes *lover* and catches hold of the 'lazy foot of Time': 'And why not the swift foot of Time? Had not that been as proper?' They are dabbing now, rather than punching or pressing, and the words suggest that contact has been achieved.

Rosalind accepts the challenge, makes a larger statement, and then offers to enumerate the 'diverse paces' of Time. She is now, gently, in command, and he is attentive. She probably stands close to him and a little out of his gaze; he may sit on the ground.

By no means, sir. Time travels in diverse paces with diverse persons. I'll tell you who Time ambles withal, who Time trots withal, who Time gallops withal, and who he stands still withal.

If she has continued to move around Orlando, she will be still by the end of this speech. Orlando is polite – 'I prithee, who doth he trot withal?' – and as Rosalind holds the stage he follows this with a series of questions which show that he listens attentively. Rosalind is prompt in reply, sharp-witted and precise; she ends each comment pointedly and may give a vocal and physical imitation of each of the varying 'paces'. Perhaps the comparative brevity of her last two replies shows that she grows bored with the recital, but it is more likely that speaking of going 'softly' and of 'sleeping' has made her voice more quiet and her bearing more gentle. Certainly Orlando's next question – 'Where dwell you, pretty youth' – suggests that they are now intimate. He is not interested in Time at all, and the speaker, not the wit, holds his attention:

ORL. I prithee, who doth he trot withal?
ROS. Marry, he trots hard with a young maid between the contract of her marriage and the day it is solemnized: if the interim be but a se'nnight, Time's pace is so hard that it seems the length of seven year.
ORL. Who ambles Time withal?
ROS. With a priest that lacks Latin and a rich man that hath not the gout; for the one sleeps easily because he cannot study, and the other lives merrily because he feels no pain; the one lacking the burden of lean and wasteful learning, the other knowing no burden of heavy tedious penury. These Time ambles withal.
ORL. Who doth he gallop withal?
ROS. With a thief to the gallows; for though he go as softly as foot can fall, he thinks himself too soon there.
ORL. Who stays it still withal?
ROS. With lawyers in vacation; for they sleep between term and term, and then they perceive not how Time moves.
ORL. Where dwell you, pretty youth?

Rosalind does not lose her head, but maintains her disguise. Only the elaboration of her replies shows that she has floated easily into a new intimacy with Orlando. But his personal question traps her and she is betrayed into a very feminine metaphor which provokes a more abrupt question:

ROS. With this shepherdess, my sister; here in the skirts of the forest, like fringe upon a petticoat.
ORL. Are you native of this place?

Her disguise is threatened by his darting question; Rosalind may stiffen momentarily, or even withdraw a little before she rallies with a rustic rejoinder – which is very far from truth: 'As the coney that you see dwell where she is kindled.' This is counter- productive and Orlando dismisses it: perhaps he looks more curiously at Ganymede than before. Rosalind evades the stronger challenge and has to think quickly to keep the lead in the conversation. She discovers a way to do so that allows her to attack and taunt Orlando until he has to break through her line of thought and press his own love: 'Fair youth, I would I could make thee believe I love' (line 357). This proves no easy resolution but, rather, releases Rosalind's own insecurities. Now it is her turn to question more closely, although she has a light touch still. Her longer phrase glides:

But, in good sooth, are you he that hangs the verses on the trees wherein Rosalind is so admired?

He swears 'by the white hand of Rosalind' that he is that lover, but this does not satisfy her. Probably he has taken her hand with these words or, at least, come much closer. The 'saucy lackey' is no longer apparent in Rosalind's speech or behaviour; she feels weak and either needs or hungers for further assurance: 'But are you so much in love as your rhymes speak?' With his reply – 'Neither rhyme nor reason can express how much' – something snaps inside her, and she cries out in both joy and fear:

Love is merely a madness; and, I tell you, deserves as well a dark house and a whip as madmen do;   . . .

In that 'I tell you', Rosalind shows that she has kept or regained her control. With this awareness of the make-believe she has the upper hand. She holds Orlando so close now that she is able to fantasise about all the lovemaking and unfaithfulness she has ever dreamed of. She can move away from him, knowing that he listens intently; she can come close to him, knowing, for the moment, that nothing can impede her excitement.

If a reader has toy figures to stand in for the speakers of this dialogue, the best way to explore its dynamics is to start by introducing too much activity. A first experiment should give Rosalind all the movements, holding Orlando still. Then this could be followed by reversing the procedure, and only when that is complete should an attempt be made to realise a full engagement, with interactions. By this time, unnecessary complications could be rejected and the scene imagined with appropriate economy.

☆

No scene can be considered properly in isolation. This is as true of its movement as it is of every other element of its theatrical life.

When strong narrative interest focusses attention keenly on a single movement or gesture, the words spoken at that moment often fail to give an adequate indication of what is happening on stage. For example, everything that an actor has enacted or imagined about Hamlet will influence the way in which he turns from the 'To be or not to be' soliloquy to 'affront' Ophelia – to use Claudius's word for the encounter:

> Thus conscience does make cowards of us all;
> And thus the native hue of resolution
> Is sicklied o'er with the pale cast of thought,
> And enterprises of great pitch and moment,
> With this regard, their currents turn awry,
> And lose the name of action. – Soft you now!
> The fair Ophelia. – Nymph, in thy orisons
> Be all my sins rememb'red.   (iii i 83–90)

The sharp changes in Hamlet's speech as he sees and speaks to Ophelia have led modern editors to use some unusual punctuation. The text printed here is typical, with a full-stop followed immediately by a dash, and then an exclamation mark and another full-stop and another dash before a further line is complete. Such flaws and starts on the printed page are signs of a theatrical crux which a reader should make a special effort to visualise.

Hamlet's soliloquy seems to finish strongly. Although he speaks of cowardice, he also imagines 'resolution' and this may well be the thought which sustains the last sentence all the way through its five and a half lines. His concluding phrase, 'And lose the name of action', seems to have a brisk energy: he might well turn away to leave the stage and set about some 'enterprise'. He would then find himself, quite suddenly, face to face with Ophelia. He would stop, even more suddenly, on 'Soft you now': he is trapped, cornered, and forced to speak. The gentleness of his words might then be false; possibly he suspects that he has walked into a trap which the King has set, and so will over-act his part for the sake of an unseen audience. His reference to his own 'sins' could be an ironic smoke-screen; he might, indeed, 'affront' Ophelia in the word's dominant senses of attack and insult. She would remain motionless, not knowing what is happening. When she does speak it is to ask how he has been all the time since she saw him last.

But, on the contrary, the earlier parts of the play may show that mental energy always leaves Hamlet physically inert. He would then finish the soliloquy gazing into space, contemplating his loss of resolution rather than the action which he has avoided. Ophelia, who has been told to 'walk' about the stage (see line 43), might have courage to move at this point and so catch Hamlet's eye; she might even choose to cross his line of vision. Either way the meeting will be at her instigation, and so Hamlet's 'Soft you know! The fair Ophelia' could indicate a pause before he is ready to speak to her: probably they are at some distance from each other. But the rest of the play may make Ophelia incapable of making any first step. She has been given a prayer book so that she can pretend to be at her devotions (see lines 45–8) and so she may be kneeling at this time, taking refuge in pretended piety. If so Hamlet could move behind her back as he spoke. It is just possible that he takes up a similar position to the one he will use later (in III iii) when he discovers Claudius at prayer. When he does address her directly, his words are gentle and sustained, full of wonder and self-reproach. He is direct at first, with 'Nymph', but then more flexible; he might take one step and then pause. So it would be Ophelia's task, with the next words, to bring about a close encounter:

> Good my lord,
> How does your honour for this many a day?

Hamlet may remain quite still for 'I humbly thank you; well, well, well', retreating into his own thoughts once more.

So the action of this scene, the bearing, movements and gestures of its two figures, can give Shakespeare's words almost opposite effects. Which is the more 'true' depends on how the whole play has been brought alive in continuous relationship to Shakespeare's text. Each person has been realised, step by step, in performance and so the dramatic excitement of this scene will carry conviction and the impression of deep involvement, below the level of speech or, even, of conscious thought. A reader must attempt a similar but imaginary realisation of the whole if such a scene is to come alive in his mind.

☆

Early scenes are usually the least ambiguous. For this reason most of the examples chosen for this and the previous chapter have been from the beginning of parts or when two persons meet for the first time. But we have seen already how the Messenger in *Much Ado* is progressively revealed during his short time on stage and how his last words and actions are the most open to different interpretations as well as giving the actor his most powerful moment on stage. We have seen how Rosencrantz and Guildenstern are tested as the play proceeds, Guildenstern showing more and more his iron hand and unsympathetic mind. The longer and more complex the part, the more this gradual revelation becomes essential to the very meaning and force of a play.

Often very few words are used for the principals in the last scenes, showing that Shakespeare trusts the actor now to present in his own way what he has discovered in his role. Rosalind, who spends most of *As You Like It* talking to almost everyone she meets, has only five lines to speak after she has shed her disguise; she must wait to regain her tongue until the illusion is broken and she steps forward to speak an Epilogue. She has not become less interesting in this last scene: the reverse is true, because the mask has dropped; but she must now hold the centre of the stage by being simply herself. In Act v of *Twelfth Night* Viola is on stage for 369 lines, but she has only 45 to speak and nothing at all to say for the last 100 – even though it is then that Orsino proposes marriage to her. After this, before Feste sings a last song, everyone on stage has to turn towards Viola to see how she reacts, how she greets Orsino and how he receives her. Only the experience of playing the whole role will show the performer how Viola makes this last contribution to the comedy.

Malvolio in the same play has three separate speeches in the last Act, the second being sufficiently long to establish him firmly at the centre of attention. But he is on stage for 32 more lines after this, and says nothing at all until he makes his exit with 'I'll be revenged on the whole pack of you' (line 364). These few words have been used in many different ways. They have been made absurd, pathetic, desperate, dignified, smug and untroubled, murderously and chillingly self-centred, practical. They have been spoken publicly and aside, loudly and quietly, quickly and slowly, in one phrase and in two. In some performances Malvolio has crossed the whole stage very deliberately before he leaves, and in others he has taken the shortest way with dangerous speed; sometimes he has staggered, as if almost blind, before being led off. Each actor makes his own choice, and the audience must judge the truth of his performance.

Any major role in Shakespeare has to be studied in sequence, because this progressive revelation of inward life is one of the main structural principles of Shakespearean drama. Towards the end of *Julius Caesar*, before the 'day is gone' and 'deeds are done' (v iii 63–4), the leaders on both sides of the contest sense that appearances are about to be put on trial and deceptions can last no longer. Octavius says that he is

> . . .   at the stake,
> And bay'd about with many enemies;   . . .

but he also knows

> And some that smile have in their hearts, I fear
> Millions of mischiefs.   (iv i 48–51)

Twenty lines later Brutus recognises that

When love begins to sicken and decay,
It useth an enforced ceremony.
There are no tricks in plain and simple faith;
But hollow men, like horses hot at hand,
Make gallant show and promise of their mettle;
But when they should endure the bloody spur,
They fall their crests, and like deceitful jades,
Sink in the trial.   . . .   (IV ii 20–7)

As horses are tested in battle, so the principal persons in a tragedy reveal
their true mettle in the last Acts. In comedy, pretences and masks drop
quite suddenly, as the plot brings everyone together at the close, but in
the history plays and tragedies it is conflict and suffering that draw the
truth out of the protagonists inch by inch; 'a bloody spur' strikes again
and again, and so makes 'trial' of manhood.

The climax of Macbeth's role is the wordless fight with Macduff.
King Lear 'knows not what he says' during most of his last moments,
and his final words are capable of many interpretations:

Do you see this? Look on her. Look, her lips.
Look there, look there!   (*Lear*, v iii 310–11)

Does he think Cordelia is alive or is he once more asserting his will? Are
these words strong or weak? The text does not tell us and each actor
must find what his performance as a whole directs him to do. Lear then
'faints' (line 311), but it is four lines later that Edgar says 'He is gone
indeed'. How much does Lear suffer or resist at the end? Is he at peace?
Has he slipped back into madness?

The theatrical excitement at the end of a play cannot be evaluated by
studying the matter of the text or the manner of its utterance, or the
actions, gestures and movement that the words imply. The drama is
expressed now in the total being of the actor, operating with heightened
sensibility and power, and totally involved. Paradoxically, where
Shakespeare seems to have given most freedom of choice, a performer
may find he has least ability to choose; it is here that, at the deepest
level, he can give only his all. The last moments draw the actor into his
role and the two become almost indistinguishable. This may have
happened before, earlier in the play; but at the end nothing less will
satisfy.

It is for this reason that many directors in present-day theatres who
give highly detailed guidance to actors and stamp their own interpretations on Shakespeare's plays, will confess that once a play is cast their
hands are tied and only a small range of possibilities can be explored. In
the experience of Trevor Nunn, Director of the Royal Shakespeare
Company:

Really 90 per cent of what happens in any given production is decided the moment the play is cast, because whatever the production approach, whatever overt production ideas emerge, the mould is cast at that moment. It is no good asking one actor to become a different kind of actor because one has had a production idea. One is working within the range of that particular actor, so if you've got the casting right in the first place, then most of the thoughts and ideas about the play are going to be communicated. If the casting is wrong nothing can save it.[1]

A reader cannot easily bring this kind of consideration to a play. It is possible to cast people one knows very well indeed into the various parts and imagine them living through the sequence of scenes; and, with great concentration, this can be a useful exercise. Actors whose work is very familiar may also be cast in this notional way. But only an experience of the process of rehearsal and of the changes that occur from one performance to another can give a true idea of the deepest demands made upon actors and the ways in which they may respond.

If a reader lives near a good theatre which has a number of 'preview performances' before an official opening night, I recommend attendance at all the previews of a new production. In this way someone who is not a member of a theatre company can see the effect of rehearsals – because they continue throughout the preview period – and also witness the actors' gradual acceptance of the full challenge of performance before an audience. The best way to use this opportunity is to concentrate attention on the leading actor or actress. I shall never forget standing at the back of the theatre to see twelve consecutive performances of *Titus Andronicus* when Laurence Olivier was developing his performance of the title role for a tour of the play throughout Europe. I saw then, in minutest detail, the excitement of acting, its truth and its dangers. This is the next best thing to being involved directly in rehearsals, and it is an opportunity open to almost everyone living within reach of a good theatre.

Another way of increasing one's ability to see what a text offers to an actor is to set about learning how an actor works. This is not easy: the effects of posture, gesture and movement are comparatively easy to visualise, but the inner processes and personal commitment of an actor can be known only by being an actor or by coming very close indeed to actors in rehearsal and performance. Any attempt to question an actor about his art will soon meet instinctive reticence or pretence or mockery, and it is better to turn to books which give a very full account of the actor's art. The most helpful of these – despite some perverseness in literary presentation – are the series of books by the Russian actor and director, Constantin Stanislavski. He confessed that his theatre, the Moscow Art Theatre at the beginning of this century, had not found an appropriate way of staging Shakespeare's plays; but this is probably an advantage to an English-speaking reader because he can forget particular textual problems and concentrate on what Stanislavski says about acting. I recommend *An Actor Prepares*, *Building a Character*, *Creating a Role* and *My Life in Art*. There are many other books on acting, but no other series that draws on such a wide experience and complete achievement, or whose author has questioned so continuously the nature of his art.

6 | *Personal Imperatives*

A further investigation is profitable when attempting to read a text from an actor's point of view. I have said that the outward elements of performance, such as gesture and movement, can be studied without any specialist knowledge. The same is true of the opposite extreme. By identifying in a very personal way with a single part and following it right through, a reader can discover at least the size of the actor's task and something of its shape. By concentrating on what happens around the chosen role, a reader encounters the developing action as an actor does and so will begin to hear and see the play afresh.

This process is distinct from the study of single role, suggested in chapter 4, which starts with the words of only one part and examines their demands on the actor. Now I propose that the reader begins by considering the whole play, but from the point of view of the chosen role. The text should be read looking outward, to see what has to be effected by the actor on other people, and inward, to realise the effect of an attempt to perform it. To assess the shape of the role, the length of each appearance on stage should be noted, and of time off-stage. It is helpful to write down, in the margin of a text, all that this one person will look at or try to avoid seeing, and to note each article or person that is touched or controlled. When the words of others are heard with such special interest that they enter into the speeches of the role, these should be marked, together with the repetitions. With such preparation, we may gain a better idea of the life of a role.

Hamlet's first entry is silent and affairs of state take place around him. When King Claudius addresses him from the throne, the summons is quick and Hamlet's response equally so:

> But now, my cousin Hamlet, and my son –
> HAM. A little more than kin, and less than kind.
> KING. How is it that the clouds still hang on you?
> HAM. Not so, my lord; I am too much in the sun. (I ii 64–7)

Having sat or stood for more than 60 lines, Hamlet is triggered into speech which is alive with puns, antitheses, contradictions. An active mind and an alert sense of himself must have prepared Hamlet and the actor for these speeches; and both must now sustain performance. Under all the earlier words in this scene – sub-textually, as Stanislavski would say – a great deal has been happening. Now Hamlet's short, direct retort silences the King; the Queen then speaks as his mother, more personally and coaxingly (using the second person singular, where Claudius had used the more formal plural mode):

> Good Hamlet, cast thy nighted colour off,
> And let thine eye look like a friend on Denmark.
> Do not for ever with thy vailed lids
> Seek for thy noble father in the dust;·   . . .

She is conscious of his clothes, his eyes, and his unspoken thoughts; she wants to be close to him, and perhaps she is. Hamlet listens, but speaks only to pick up a single word and challenge her use of it:

> Thou know'st 'tis common – all that lives must die,
> Passing through nature to eternity.
> HAM. Ay, madam, it is common.
> QU.   If it be,
> Why seems it so particular with thee?

Now Hamlet is stung more deeply and seizes hold of 'seems'. Then he controls himself and speaks at greater length, with firmly structured phrases:

> Seems, madam! Nay, it is; I know not seems.
> 'Tis not alone my inky cloak, good mother,
> Nor customary suits of solemn black,
> Nor windy suspiration of forc'd breath,
> No, nor the fruitful river in the eye,
> Nor the dejected haviour of the visage,
> Together with all forms, moods, shapes of grief,
> That can denote me truly. These, indeed, seem;
> For they are actions that a man might play;
> But I have that within which passes show –
> These but the trappings and the suits of woe.   (76–85)

Neither his words nor appearance nor actions can tell all about his feelings, his consciousness of what is happening around and within him. The Queen says nothing more until the King has argued at some length with her son; and then Hamlet replies simply – 'I shall in all my best obey you, madam' – and is silent again until everyone has left the crowded stage and he is alone. This first episode requires the actor of Hamlet to maintain an active sense of himself, of which his words give only hints – and even those sharpened by a sense of performance: for Hamlet has an actor's ability to seem what he is not, and the actor who plays the role must establish these two levels of illusion.

The soliloquy which follows is a more direct and uncensored expression of thoughts and feelings, but it breaks down several times into mere exclamation. The rein of communicable thought barely controls his racing, soaring and plunging sensations, even though at times a gentle and careful tone intervenes. The soliloquy comes to an end immediately before the arrival of Horatio, Marcellus and Bernardo. Either Hamlet is suddenly aware of someone approaching and so stops speaking, or they enter just as he is about to leave the stage so that the entry is one of those strokes of fate that will accompany his progress through the play. Either way, he hesitates before greeting Horatio by name, again having to create a performance adjusted to the demands of the people around him.

From now on Hamlet has much to learn. Soon he is on the battlements at night, wrapped up against the extreme cold. He hears the King's celebrations off-stage and waits for what he has been told is his father's ghost. Soon the actor of Hamlet is fully stretched as he meets the new demands thrust upon him. Hamlet is ready to trust his life to the Ghost's beckoning; he cries out in pain; he speaks 'wild and whirling words' (i v 133). Yet he also has moments of very simple and deliberate speech – 'It is an honest ghost, that let me tell you' (i v 138) – and begins to act the 'antic disposition' which he intends to use as a grotesque concealment of his real thoughts when he returns to court. Now he does not question his involvement:

> The time is out of joint. O cursed spite,
> That ever I was born to set it right!   (i v 189–90)

But he is aware that he has to appear more at ease than he is. He does not leave until he has assumed a more casual performance and rejoined the others, with 'Nay, come let's go together'. Again the actor of Hamlet must be able to play two parts, simultaneously: this time the gentle friend overlays the passionate reformer.

The actor has ten or fifteen minutes before returning to the stage. He enters silent and reading a book, but his clothes are worn as if he were a madman; the Queen introduces him with 'look where sadly the poor wretch comes reading' (ii ii 167). Such is the beginning of a scene in which Hamlet is on-stage for 440 consecutive lines. It is his longest scene and in many ways his most relaxed. He takes his own time to taunt Polonius, greet Rosencrantz and Guildenstern, perform for them all and, then, encounter the Players and perform for them. He presses questions but is then free to move away quickly to new and contrary matters.

This long scene with all its opportunities for varied performance is also the actor's opportunity to explore the most personal elements of his role and so establish himself in the audience's confidence. Those who listen are relaxed by laughter and alerted by moments of danger, while the actor of Hamlet controls pace, tone, intensity, rhythm. He has to make deliberate choices, time and again, according to his inner sense of the role he plays. Hamlet speaks repeatedly of his father, mother and uncle, and of the nation he was born to lead. He speaks, too, of his earlier life, and this is the first scene in which he refers to Ophelia, whom the audience has seen acknowledging his love and suffering for it. He sometimes acts the madman, but that feeds and releases his fantasy, so that performance becomes reality and he expresses a deep sense of himself and his destiny. Hamlet holds centre-stage throughout except for the First Player's sensational account of Pyrrhus seeking vengeance among the flames of Troy. It is immediately after this that Hamlet sends every one else away so that he can be 'alone' (II ii 542). So this free and open scene ends with a soliloquy in which Hamlet speaks specifically as an actor and in this way draws the audience's interest forward once more. What will the play's action, and his own ability to perform with truth, prompt the hero to do?

Hamlet's next appearance is for the intensely self-questioning 'To be or not to be' soliloquy and for a face-to-face encounter with Ophelia, in which his pain and passion threaten to overwhelm him. He probably rushes from the stage but then returns only 27 lines later in full and precise command as he instructs the Players in the 'temperance' needed for the operation of their art. From now on, until the end of Act IV scene iv, when he soliloquises after seeing Fortinbras's army, Hamlet is caught up in action that demands quick releases of energy and a whole series of precise and powerful re-actions. There is some relief from activity while the Mousetrap is performed by the Players, but Hamlet is alert and inwardly excited all the time as he watches both play and audience. He leaves the stage five times during this central passage of the play, but always returns immediately, three times within one minute. The most sustained encounter with a single person is with his mother, but during those 210 lines he also kills Polonius and is visited by his father's ghost.

Act III and the first part of Act IV are the active centre of Hamlet's role. There are moments of great delicacy, especially with Ophelia and his mother, and some calm and even methodical speeches, but the highlights are outbursts of rage, passion and savage humour. The actor needs a full measure of that 'temperance' which Hamlet recommended to the Players if he is not to 'o'erstep the modesty of nature' and 'make

the judicious grieve' (III ii 18–28). However gently and courteously the
meeting with Ophelia begins, it reaches its climax with:

> . . . You jig and amble, and you lisp, and nickname God's creatures, and
> make your wantonness your ignorance. Go to, I'll no more on't; it hath made
> me mad. I say we will have no more marriage: those that are married
> already, all but one, shall live; the rest shall keep as they are. To a nunnery,
> go.   (III i 145–50)

As the Mousetrap is performed, Hamlet can scarcely wait for its horrific
climax:

> . . .   Begin, murderer; pox, leave thy damnable faces and begin. Come; the
> croaking raven doth bellow for revenge.   (III ii 246–8)

When Claudius rises from his throne and leaves the stage, Hamlet calls
out 'What, frighted with false fire!' (line 260) and then declaims:

> Why, let the strucken deer go weep,
>   The hart ungallèd play;
> For some must watch, while some must sleep;
>   Thus runs the world away.   . . .   (III ii 265–8)

This seems the more strange and elated in that Hamlet has enough self-
awareness to know that such behaviour fits an actor who wears a 'forest
of feathers'. When he is called to his mother's closet, he 'starts' wildly
and taunts the messengers. His pulse races strongly until he is alone and
knows

> . . .   Now could I drink hot blood
> And do such bitter business as the day
> Would quake to look on.   . . .   (380–2)

He leaves the stage to return unexpectedly within a few minutes;
Claudius is praying and for a moment it looks as if Hamlet will kill him
impulsively. He recovers control only to wait for a more suitable time

> When he is drunk asleep, or in his rage;
> Or in th' incestuous pleasure of his bed;   . . .   (III iii 89–90)

A murder that might send his victim to heaven is not 'horrid' enough to
satisfy Hamlet's passion, and he leaves to go to his mother.

On his very entrance Gertrude thinks he means to murder her.
Polonius responds to her cry for help and Hamlet kills him, probably

with a single stab. He forces Gertrude to sit down and proceeds to terrify her with his words. She tries to restrain him:

> What have I done that thou dar'st wag thy tongue
> In noise so rude against me? (III iv 39–40)

and again:

>   Ay me, what act,
> That roars so loud and thunders in the index? (51–2)

Soon Hamlet is denouncing Claudius with passionate reiterations. He is stopped only by the appearance of his father's ghost. Then he no longer 'roars' but is close to tears (see line 130), and his mother can be tender with him; and so, briefly, he is able to be tender too. But Hamlet's mind is soon drawn back to what he has done and what he must do. The scene ends with such renewed energy that Hamlet has no respect for Polonius's corpse: 'I'll lug the guts into the neighbour room' (line 212).

Short scenes follow. When armed men are sent to apprehend Hamlet, he is defiant, mocking and spirited:

> . . .   The King is a thing –
> GUILD. A thing, my lord!
> HAMLET Of nothing. Bring me to him. Hide fox, and all after. (IV ii 28–30)

Brought face to face with Claudius, he continues to mock him, insisting on calling him 'My mother' – since 'man and wife is one flesh' – and leaving abruptly to go to England. But he is back on stage again to catch sight of Fortinbras's army marching 'softly' and in good order (IV iv 8) towards battle. Hamlet sees this as a criticism of his own behaviour, but in this moment of reconsideration he does not regret his own impulsive actions; rather he blames himself for inaction, and concludes:

> . . .   O, from this time forth,
> My thoughts be bloody, or be nothing worth! (IV iv 65–6)

The irony is that Hamlet is still talking of vengeance and not achieving it; but the search for passionate commitment, the restless energy and the extravagant words are all at full tide still.

In one of the few quiet and sustained passages in this central section of the play, Hamlet has spoken to Horatio:

>   for thou hast been
> As one, in suff'ring all, that suffers nothing;
> A man that Fortune's buffets and rewards
> Hast ta'en with equal thanks; and blest are those
> Whose blood and judgment are so well comeddled
> That they are not a pipe for Fortune's finger
> To sound what stop she please. Give me that man
> That is not passion's slave, and I will wear him
> In my heart's core, ay, in my heart of heart,
> As I do thee.   . . .   (III ii 63–72)

Only if the actor is secure in the 'heart's core' of his performance can the part of Hamlet be played – as he himself insisted that the players should – without 'mouthing it' or being 'too tame' for what the text requires. If the challenge is not ducked and the actor takes upon himself all the pretence, exaggeration, insecurity, instability, suffering, drive, passion and violence of the long central passage, anything can happen; and with a single misjudgement the drama can begin to slip helplessly into mere sound and fury. At a deep and secret level of the actor's consciousness, 'judgement' must always be comeddled with 'blood'. Hamlet is a dangerous role, and that is part of the play's fascination; its performance must have an unseen strength and coherence. The audience can sense this subliminally.

The deepest level of consciousness is shown more openly in the last major section of the part. Hamlet has been absent from the stage for more than twenty minutes, so the actor has had time to regain energy, take stock, and adjust himself for the next set of demands. Although he is rejoined by the steady Horatio, with whom he has not been seen since the play-within-the-play, Hamlet moves at once into new territory. He meets a gravedigger who, by an obvious and shocking stroke of fate, had started making graves 'that very day that young Hamlet was born' (v i 143). Hamlet is as much at ease and in control as when he had met Rosencrantz and Guildenstern, but now his thoughts are led by the clown's songs and skulls to a review of his earliest life and a prevision of his own death, besides those of fools, ladies and potentates. Then the whole court enters, following Ophelia's corpse, and Hamlet is impelled to make two ringing affirmations that in the context can carry a sense of absolute, deeply personal truth: 'This is I, Hamlet the Dane' and 'I lov'd Ophelia' (v i 251–2 and 263).

Between these two unequivocal public statements, Hamlet fights with Laertes, Ophelia's brother, using naked hands:

>   Why, I will fight with him upon this theme
>   Until my eyelids will no longer wag.   (v i 260–1)

With passionate commitment he is still ready for endless and violent action, and the two young men have to be pulled apart. After the Queen has intervened, Hamlet is quieter and leaves the stage with mockery and defiance:

> Let Hercules himself do what he may,
> The cat will mew, and dog will have his day. (285–6)

The actor has very little time, because Hamlet is back again after only seven lines and recounts to Horatio all his actions since leaving for England. But he looks ahead now with a new sense of moral justification:

> . . .   is't not perfect conscience
> To quit him with this arm? And is't not to be damn'd
> To let this canker of our nature come
> In further evil? (v ii 67–70)

As he faces danger now, Hamlet sounds steady and deeply reflective:

> HOR. If your mind dislike anything, obey it. I will forestall their repair hither, and say you are not fit.
> HAM. Not a whit, we defy augury: there is a special providence in the fall of a sparrow. If it be now, 'tis not to come; if it be not to come, it will be now; if it be not now, yet it will come – the readiness is all. Since no man owes of aught he leaves, what is't to leave betimes? Let be. (v ii 209–16)

This is almost the reverse of 'Now could I drink hot blood . . . ' and is the more impressive in that Hamlet has just responded spiritedly, with quickest invention, to Osric's courtly double-talk and to a second Messenger's more urgent query.

So when the stage fills once more with the King, the Queen and the whole court, the audience, as well as the actor, knows that the end has come. The courtesies and formalities of the duel hold tense attention and every move that Hamlet makes will be scrutinised closely. Then, after three bouts, Laertes wounds Hamlet as he stands relaxed and unsuspecting. At once both are incensed and in a remarkably short time all the deaths follow: Gertrude, Laertes, Claudius (killed three different ways) and Hamlet. In this last, strenuous action, with tension heightened by a sense of destiny and responsibility, and by danger, haste, hatred, moral indignation and love, the actor has to draw on all his resources. All his careful study of the part, all his experience and instinct as an actor – and all his wits, imagination and courage as a man – are called into the reckoning; and this is at a time when the long and demanding performance has already drawn out all but his last resources. Shakespeare has helped by providing the slower encounters with the Gravedigger, Horatio and young Osric to prepare the way, and give opportunity for defining and sharpening crucial elements of the performance. But at last the actor has to trust the moment.

When the audience enters the theatre, it knows that Hamlet will die, but neither audience nor actor knows exactly how he will do so. (And this is true, even in well-drilled twentieth-century productions in which almost nothing is left to chance.) There are precise and resonant words in the last moments of the play, but as Hamlet is dying much of what he says involves very short sentences open to a wide range of meanings and implications: '. . . I follow thee. – I am dead, Horatio. – Wretched queen, adieu! . . . O, I could tell you – But let it be. – Horatio, I am dead;' . . . 'O, I die, Horatio! . . . The rest is silence.'

After the exertion of the fight and killings, and after the long journey towards this moment which has lasted the whole play, the actor will discover, in the quick forge of imaginative thought and in his physical involvement in the drama, just how these words ring out. His work in rehearsal will be tested and perhaps transformed. The unnecessary has no place here; subterfuge, pretence and a show of the hero as actor have almost disappeared. The excitement of the play has led towards this and is summed up in this, as the audience shares the actor's discovery and achievement in the moment of creation.

☆

If we wish to read one of Shakespeare's plays with an awareness of its theatrical life, we must be prepared to enter into its various roles with the patience, skill and imagination of an actor. We must see and hear and feel. Time, space, human beings and ever-changing encounters must all enter into our response. And beyond this, we must recognise how Shakespeare suggests several levels of being at a single moment, so that in one person thoughts may be both quick and slow, conscious and unconscious, deliberate and instinctive. We must also be prepared to venture beyond what we have foreseen or imagined as the play leads to those moments that put every element of a performance at risk.

We should be very wary of character-analysis and the reduction of a play to meanings or the treatment of themes. The first task is to respond more adequately to a lively image of abundant and challenging life.

7 | *Shakespeare's Text*

At one time I thought that my first chapter would be about the words of Shakespeare's plays as they have survived in early printed books and as modern editors present them to us. All our study and enjoyment must start from this evidence and any opinions we form have to be brought back to the same source for assessment. But I decided later to place discussion of Shakespeare's text at the half-way mark because, until a reader has developed a sense of the plays in performance, a text cannot be read as it should be: only a few difficulties will be identified, and the positive clues to Shakespeare's image of life will pass unregarded. A literary reading can place barriers in the way of understanding which are difficult to eradicate later. Once a play begins to have a lively enactment in our imaginations, we return to the text with new and sharpened curiosity.

New problems arise in plenty, and one in particular. Already in this book we may have stopped in our tracks to ask whether we were not being too ingenious and trying to wring too much from the words on the printed page. Does a search for theatrical life lead us to study the text with too great a finesse? Would a working dramatist, whose practice was to write two new plays for each new season, write with such great care and detailed awareness? I think there are three answers to this which, together, are conclusive.

First, we must remember that to create and to judge are two very different functions. In the 'quick forge and working-house' of composition (*Henry V*, v Prol. 23), ideas and images combine at white heat from all parts of the writer's mind and, in due course and proportion, our own imaginative enjoyment may have something of the same excitement. But when we try to check and evaluate our reactions, a more painstaking attention is necessary. The more we have been caught up in imaginative re-creation, the more complex will be the later task of critical comprehension. But there is recompense: the attempt to explain, verify and evaluate stretches our minds and imagination, so that we develop stronger and more open responses for the next imaginative encounter.

Secondly, we should remember that, while Shakespeare had a teeming imagination, it is equally true that he wrote with great care. Ben Jonson repeated the actors' tale that he used to deliver manuscripts without a single line being 'blotted out' or corrected, adding that

He was, indeed, honest, and of an open and free nature: had an excellent fantasy, brave notions and gentle expression, wherein he flowed with that facility that sometime it was necessary he should be stopped.   . . .[1]

But Jonson had no doubt that Shakespeare 'redeemed his vices with his virtues'.

I have already quoted the verses prefixed to the 1623 Folio in which Jonson speaks of Shakespeare striking a 'second heat upon the Muses' anvil' and involving himself totally in the act of creation:

>   . . .   Look how the father's face
> Lives in his issue; even so, the race
> Of Shakespeare's mind and manners brightly shines
> In his well-turnéd and true-filéd lines;
> In each of which he seems to shake a lance,
> As brandished at the eyes of ignorance.   . . .

However fluently Shakespeare wrote, his 'living lines' were deeply wrought and highly finished, and they can merely dazzle a careless reader. We may respond quickly to their vitality, but their secrets are not discovered easily.

Thirdly, the pleasures of careful attention to the script of a play, and the way in which this leads on and on in a process of discovery, is the most convincing reason why we should be prepared for meticulous study and precise enquiry. Like Shakespeare, we should be imaginative *and* fastidious: 'of an open and free nature', but also as 'honest' as we are able. The words on the page become an inexhaustible mine from which we quarry an imaginative wealth which becomes our own in the taking.

Some academics believe that they are the only honest students of Shakespeare. In their view, actors and directors see only what they wish to see, and then pass quickly on to consider how they can develop these perceptions in the creation of strong, attractive and idiosyncratic stage productions. So Professor Burckhardt has complained that

There is an odd superstition abroad that nothing can be part of Shakespeare's intention that cannot be communicated directly across the footlights. First and foremost, we are told, he was a 'man of the theatre'; the implication is that what we see when we see a play of his acted is the unmediated thing itself. Of course this is nonsense; what we see is an interpretation . . . . A large part of such an interpretation is subliminal; the stage action expresses it only by indirection. Unfortunately, this subliminal interpretation is often also undisciplined and irresponsible, dictated by vanity, desire for effect or novelty, misunderstanding, or even sheer ignorance.[2]

The truth is that a scholar can be just as 'undisciplined and irresponsible' as the 'man of the theatre'. He may pursue his very own theories about Shakespeare's 'meaning' without regard for those elements of the text which awaken sensitive and lifelike performances. But good scholars, like good actors, are honest, patient and painstaking. The complications and niceties of Shakespeare's dialogue encourage these virtues in all students, theatrical and academic, and never more strongly than when they bring their own 'fantasy, brave notions and gentle expressions' to the encounter. The task of re-creating the plays, either in a reader's imagination or on the stage, raises searching questions about a text which lead on to careful dissection and enquiry. Absolutely everything counts: what is there in the text, what is missing, and what may be suggested.

☆

The nature of the evidence, as it was first printed and as we read it today, must be considered very carefully. First we should face the question of authenticity: is this what Shakespeare himself wrote? Sometimes we have to answer that we do not know. For example, in the previous chapter we noticed how Hamlet arrives at his last dangerous and revealing moments through a series of less pressured encounters. The preparation is completed in talk with Horatio:

> If it be now, 'tis not to come; if it be not to come, it will be now; if it be not
> now, yet it will come – the readiness is all. Since no man owes of aught he
> leaves, what is't to leave betimes? Let be.   (v ii 207–10)

Most of these words could hardly be simpler, but the phrase 'Since no man owes of aught he leaves' raises obvious questions. Here Hamlet's thought takes a new line, after the conclusive 'the readiness is all'. With the new idea and new rhythm, Hamlet considers himself alongside other men and goes back to the notion that a moment of decision, and probably of death, is about to occur 'betimes' or almost 'now'. He has come to think of possession and loss. Or has he? At this point the printed evidence is very uncertain. The *second* single-volume, paperbound edition, which was probably printed from Shakespeare's own manuscript and is known now as the 'Good Quarto', reads:

since no man of ought he leaves, knows what ist to leave betimes, let be.

Peter Alexander's edition (from which I have quoted in this book, and reproduced in the first version of the passage given here) dismisses this Good Quarto reading and borrows something from the different reading of the first collected, or 'Folio', edition of 1623, viz.:

since no man ha's ought of what he leaves. What is't to leave betimes?

But notice that Professor Alexander has retained the Good Quarto's 'let be' and modified the punctuation. Professor Kitteredge attempted to make sense of the Quarto in another way:

Since no man knows aught of what he leaves, what is't to leave betimes? Let be.

Professor Sisson opted for:

Since no man of aught he leaves knows, what is't to leave betimes? Let be.

My own preference would be close to the Folio:

Since no man has aught of what he leaves, what is't to leave betimes? Let be.

In this reading 'has', rather than 'knows', accentuates the new idea of dispossession.

Almost every editor, no matter how closely he adheres to the better sense of the Folio, keeps the 'Let be' from the Quarto. But even here we should be wary. The Good Quarto has a comma and not a full stop before this phrase. Did Shakespeare punctuate as a talker not as a grammarian, so that his manuscript omitted the question mark? This could imply that, in Shakespeare's creating mind, Hamlet's involvement in questions ebbs slowly, even as he is phrasing one? Or is the comma in the Quarto text the error of a compositor working in the printing-house? This is the most likely supposition and implies that 'Let be', for all its brevity, is the representation of another entirely new thought. Then difficulty centres on how the words should be spoken. There is no stage-direction to help. Hamlet could speak to Horatio or to himself. The two words might be spoken quite sharply or, possibly, humorously in self-defence or self-disparagement. Try saying 'Let be' quietly and then loudly, slowly and then quickly, with a rising inflection and then a falling, after a long pause or immediately after the previous words. The very short sentence, varied by these mechanical means, can suggest very different reactions. Is the phrase part of Shakespeare's text or should we follow the Folio and omit it? Did Shakespeare's manuscript indicate a quick and light delivery, following the previous words with almost no pause? Or is the actor free to make the new thought register according to his own enactment of the role?

Even among the simple words of this passage, actual meanings and implications must be watched. *Owes*, in the sense of 'possesses', is obsolete today; and a reader will find himself consulting editorial annotations or a glossary to learn that the modern meaning of 'being indebted for' was no more common than the earlier sense that seems to be implied here. Attention to the authenticity of a text is inextricably involved with questions of meaning.

Common usage of the time is perhaps the greatest unknown of all when encountering Shakespeare's text for the first time. His written language was influenced by everyday talk, public pronouncements, literary traditions, and class, age and regional distinctions, as well as by the hugely complicated history of his own developing use of language, in both his personal and his literary lives. The words we read have lost some resonances and gained others; they have changed meanings, lost meanings and gained new ones. Their sound has altered, too. In studying Shakespeare we need great patience if we are to assess each word as carefully as we should.

A passage that we have considered before illustrates this:

> And enterprises of great pitch and moment,
> With this regard, their currents turn awry
> And lose the name of action. – Soft you now!
> The fair Ophelia. – Nymph, in thy orisons
> Be all my sins rememb'red.

> (*Hamlet*, III i 86–90)

Considered objectively, as 'dead' evidence on the page, some of the simplest words should puzzle us. In Shakespeare's day, *Soft you* was used as an exclamation to enjoin silence and to prevent hasty action; the second sense, which is less familiar to us, is clear in *Twelfth Night* (I v 277), *The Comedy of Errors* (III ii 69) and elsewhere in the plays. The phrase could also enjoin secrecy and concealment. So Hamlet's first thought on seeing Ophelia may be to delay or actually to prevent a meeting, and not, as we might judge from modern usage, to give expression to an instinctive surge of gentle feelings.

But then, in proverbial usage, *soft* was linked with *fair*, in the phrase *soft and fair*, meaning 'gently, peaceably'; there is a clear instance of this in *Much Ado About Nothing* (v iv 72). So we must consider that the words *fair Ophelia* might come to Hamlet's mind as a quibble on 'Soft you', and this, together with alliteration, could imply a quickening sense of wonder and delight which overcomes the first defensive reaction. On the other hand, both quibble and alliteration could represent a biting irony that follows directly from the need to hide from Ophelia in the dangerous political environment of Elsinore.

Punctuation must also be considered here. The exclamation mark of the edition I have quoted is found in neither Good Quarto nor Folio. Both these texts have a comma and this may remind us that only the slightest pause is necessary after *now*. Further enquiry will tell us that the compositor who set the type for the Good Quarto from Shakespeare's manuscript was in the habit of adding to the punctuation of his copy, not lightening it.[3]

So we may move on to the next questions, which must be 'Why *Nymph?*' and 'Why *orisons?*' Neither word was common in such a context, in theatrical or in everyday usage. Shakespeare used *nymph* in three ways: first, with reference to spirits, not mortals; second, in pastoral settings where a lover is totally enamoured of his lady; and thirdly, when he wished to suggest a strong and obvious sexual attraction. The last is the most unusual, but Hamlet's immediate reference to *sins* might imply that this is the sense required here, especially as Ophelia is no spirit and Elsinore no pastoral solitude. The sexual senses of *nymph* are found in the courtly settings of *Titus Andronicus*:

> ...   To wanton with this queen,
> This goddess, this Semiramis, this nymph,
> This siren that will charm Rome's Saturnine, ...   (ii i 21–3)

and in *Richard III*:

> ...   and want love's majesty
> To strut before a wanton ambling nymph;   ...   (i i 16–17)

Orisons is still more difficult to place exactly. By the year 1600 its archaic and poetic suggestions were already fairly established. Certainly Shakespeare used *prayers* rather than *orisons* on almost every occasion when both might have been suitable; and *devotions* is far more common in his plays than *orisons*. In association with *nymph*, some touch of unreality seems to be implied; but an alternative reading might find the edge of sarcasm in both words, especially since the syntax brings them together at the beginning of Hamlet's words to Ophelia, and the metre tends to distinguish them from the rest of the sentence. Shakespeare used *orisons* on four other occasions only, and in three of these the word is heavy with sarcasm or irony: when Queen Margaret taunts the Duke of York who is her prisoner and is being humiliated (*2 Henry VI*, I ix 110); when Henry the Fifth taunts Sir Thomas Grey who has professed loyal piety as he prepares to assassinate his king (*Henry V*, II ii 53); and when Juliet pretends that she will pray before marrying Paris (*Romeo*, IV iii 3). Only for Imogen's anxious fantasies about the absent Posthumous did Shakespeare use *orisons* without a clear edge of mockery, and here a measure of unreality is unmistakeable. 'Nymph in thy orisons . . . ' would be unique in Shakespeare's writings if it were a tender, heartfelt *and* real communication.

Word-order, syntax and metre are further important clues to dramatic meaning. Why start with the single word *Nymph*, why *orisons* so early and why *rememb'red* last? And why the passive construction? Does Hamlet think first of his own *sins*, and is this the reason why he speaks at all? Why is the rhythm of the concluding line controlled so firmly by the four leading monosyllables, with a regular iambic stress on *all* and *sins*? Why '*all* my sins'? Does Hamlet think of his sins because he supposes, either mockingly or tenderly, that Ophelia must be at her devotions in order to beg forgiveness for her own? Or for *his*?

These few words can suggest many and various enactments. For the moment, Hamlet could respond to Ophelia as an innocent and beautiful girl, and so speak gently and with reverence. The mellifluous phrasing and falling rhythms seem to support this. Or he could wince from the sight of her, suspecting some new corruption or deceit, and so speak scornfully and in self-defence. Biting stress on '*fair Ophelia*' and '*all* my *sins*', which would chime with the first regular stresses of the iambic lines, could support this. It may be, however, that Hamlet is pretending to be mad, as he had promised that he would, and so expresses a distraction of his own mind in an exaggerated mixture of gentleness and sarcasm. Or, for the moment, does Hamlet stand quite lost?

Of course, as we have seen already, the context of this encounter, and its place in a living performance of the play, will influence the meaning of this short speech. The physical distance of the two performers, their postures and relationships, will be important elements of this. Try calling these words as if communicating at some distance, and then speaking in a low voice as if Hamlet stands just behind a kneeling Ophelia. Speak them as you become suddenly tense, and then when you are excited; and then in a wholly relaxed state.

Perhaps the most persistent puzzle in Shakespeare's texts is the absence of stage-directions. Position on stage can be crucial to the meaning of the words, and to the very action of the play. A crux of this importance occurs just before the passage we have been examining. The King is arranging with the Queen and Polonius for Hamlet to 'affront' Ophelia, and says

> Sweet Gertrude, leave us too;
> For we have closely sent for Hamlet hither,
> That he, as 'twere by accident, may here
> Affront Ophelia.
> Her father and myself – lawful espials –
> Will so bestow ourselves that, seeing unseen,
> We may of their encounter frankly judge,
> And gather by him, as he is behav'd,
> If 't be the affliction of his love or no
> That thus he suffers for.   (III i 28–37)

Ophelia is on stage when all this is being spoken, but she could be out of earshot while the King speaks privately to the Queen: she might be engaged in talk with her father which no one else can hear. If the King's words do communicate to Ophelia, she will know that everything she says to Hamlet when they meet will be heard instantly by the King and her own father; then their encounter will be different from what it would be if she has not heard. Does she think that her father *is* 'at home' when she says he is? Or is she aware, at that moment, that he is actually present and eavesdropping? Does the brevity of her speeches indicate a full heart or a resolute deception? How tender is her speech, how brave, how tentative or how hollow? The mute language of the way she looks at Hamlet, when he speaks to her, will have divergent meanings according to whether she does or does not know that the King is there.

The text is not clear on this issue. The Queen continues:

> I shall obey you;
> And for your part, Ophelia, I do wish
> That your good beauties be the happy cause
> Of Hamlet's wildness: . . .

All depends on whether Gertrude moves away from Claudius on 'I shall obey you' and waits until she has reached Ophelia before continuing with, 'And for your part, Ophelia', or whether she does not move because Ophelia is so close that she has heard everything. The fact that Polonius speaks next to Ophelia, and not to the King, may indicate that the first alternative is correct and that he has been standing aside with his daughter while Claudius has taken Gertrude to the other extremity of the stage. The argument is nicely balanced because Gertrude seems to continue a single line of thought with 'And for your part, Ophelia . . . .'. I do not know for sure which stage-direction is required. I can only add that the part of Ophelia is very difficult to play if she does, indeed, know everything.

For my present purpose the investigation of this short passage has gone far enough, and perhaps too far. Only when a reader explores a text for himself, openly and in detail, asking questions about the play in performance, seeing each part from within and using his own imagination, will the worth and excitment of such an exploration be established. What can appear complicated and specialised is found then to be an adventurous game, much more accessible than bridge, or crosswords, or learning a foreign language. Our own creativity is set in action with Shakespeare's text, under his instigation and guidance. Some simple rules have to be followed – the most important have been considered already – and then all is open, and we can, if we wish, use more sophisticated means of improving our play.

Very early in any investigation, a reader must enquire about the authenticity of the text he is using. A modern edition in a separate volume will provide a textual introduction to each play explaining the nature of the 'copy' from which it was first printed, the differences between early editions where more than one exists, and how the modern editor has compiled his own text. If the reader uses a copy of the *Complete Works*, he should also consult a modern, single-volume edition for this information, although that will not explain his own editor's procedures. Alternatively, he should turn to Sir Walter W. Greg's *The Shakespeare First Folio: Its Bibliographical and Textual History* (1955, and many times reprinted). More than twenty years' work of a whole school of 'bibliographical' textual scholarship is drawn together in this book which shows the varying authority of all the early editions. An excellent summary is provided on pages 426–32 and this should be studied to place the introductions of single-volume editions in a wider perspective.

In his life-time and in the years immediately following, Shakespeare's plays were printed from many different kinds of manuscript and from corrected or supplemented copies of earlier editions. The best of 'Good Quarto' editions and the best texts in the Folio Collected edition of 1623 were printed directly from his own manuscripts. These varied from comparatively rough drafts to careful 'fair copies'. Occasionally Shakespeare's manuscript was edited for the printer by some other hand, after comparison with a prompt-book or alternative version. A professional scrivener was sometimes used to make a new manuscript for the printer, from Shakespeare's papers or from the actors' prompt-book; this copyist might well punctuate to please himself or introduce new arrangements for the stage-directions or speech-prefixes. A few plays were printed from a prompt-book, or a transcript of one, and so record modifications that the players had introduced to Shakespeare's original. Six were first published in Quartos for which the printers used unauthorised versions taken down by dictation from actors and possibly augmented by shorthand or other notes taken during performance. Although these 'bad' texts are obviously deficient in sense and metre, they sometimes have illuminating stage-directions and alternative readings that correct errors in better texts. The Quartos of *Richard III* and *King Lear* are probably reconstructions, the former from the collective memory of the company of players and the latter from some careless or botched copy of authoritative papers. Numerous texts in the Folio were printed from copies of earlier Quarto editions which had been edited with or without reference to a prompt-book or some other manuscript version now completely lost.

The story of how Shakespeare's plays came to be printed is highly complicated and can never be fully known. In contrast to many other dramatists (such as Ben Jonson and John Webster, who supplied authoritative manuscripts and visited the printing-house to check and correct the printing), Shakespeare seems to have taken very little trouble to ensure that his plays were published as accurately as possible. For each play a reader should enquire about its textual history and so understand how far the text he uses can be trusted, and what is the value of the alternative readings which he will find noted in the collations provided in most single-volume editions. When all allowances are made for the difficulties and accidents of Elizabethan publication, we and Shakespeare have been fortunate: within definable limits, when we read a modern text we are close to his manuscripts or some transcript of them.

Such reassurance can be taken only so far, however. We should be aware that there *are* many cruxes and some longer passages – and these in plays that are frequently performed and studied – where we can never be very sure of the text's authenticity. Moreover, in the last fifty years a great deal has been learnt about the compositors who set the original editions. As was mentioned earlier in this chapter in connection with the Good Quarto of *Hamlet*, we know now that, as a matter of course, they altered punctuation, and also spelling, to suit their own habits or convenience. We are thus now aware that we can never be sure of the authenticity of the original texts in these respects. Shortage of type – dramatic texts need many more marks of punctuation than others – or the need to fit 'copy' into a fixed number of pages, or the rapid correction of errors that were obvious on quick perusal of a proof sheet, or the misreading of 'copy', hasty work, carelessness, inexperience, bad light, broken type, faulty distribution of type, and many other accidents, would introduce further small alterations of this sort on almost every page. In ordinary circumstances, these minor changes introduced by compositors and chance would not be very significant, but for Shakespeare's plays, which must be searched for the tiniest clues of their implied stage-life, they are a continual source of insecurity and perplexity. The changes to punctuation, introduced by habit and error or for ease of working, throw a veil between a reader and Shakespeare's intentions that is always present and often inpenetrable. A great deal of work has been done on type-shortages, press-work and compositorial habits, but much more remains to be done, using computers and elaborate photographic devices, before any real progress can be achieved. For the present time and for years to come, a reader should maintain a total scepticism about the punctuation of any text he reads, whether original or edited. Metrical considerations can often show how faulty verse-lining or the confusion of verse and prose should be corrected, but there is little to help us to tackle the persistent problems of punctuation.

Modern editors usually punctuate to reveal the syntax as clearly as possible to a silent reader. This practice gives a cool and synthetic impression which is far from the dynamics of thought and speech. The experiment of reading aloud will show that the grammatical punctuation which is clear on the page can be laboured and metrically confusing in stage performance. Before rehearsals begin some theatre directors have the whole play typed out afresh, using only the very minimum of punctuation – chiefly full stops to separate the sentences – so that the actors and themselves will speak the text without interference from the ancient and modern punctuation which has replaced the dramatist's and removed it from our sight for ever. I recommend the exercise of making such a transcript as a means of becoming aware of this very pervasive problem. A highly dramatic episode or a long soliloquy offers the most revealing material. With the punctuation thus reduced to a minimum, a further exercise would be to speak the words in various ways so that they are metrically satisfying and make sense in the developing situation. Then new punctuation could be added to the transcript to represent the preferred reading.

Such work leads inevitably to a consideration of verse-lining, and here a reader is on surer ground. Infinite variations are possible in an actor's response to the metre, but the division of a text into lines is usually beyond reasonable doubt and provides most useful and continuous instruction for an actor. The importance of verse-lining is most obvious in the occurence of incomplete or half-lines which indicate pauses or hesitations, and are the equivalent of stage-directions from

Shakespeare himself. Many modern editors have failed to grasp their significance and arrange the text on the printed page so that their presence is obscured, and some actors do not bother to follow their promptings. A few examples will show how verse-lining can help a reader's search for the stage-life of a play.

The Tragedy of Othello, with its intense and intimate scenes, illustrates this particularly well – for example, this exchange between Desdemona and Emilia:

EM.	Alas, what does this gentleman conceive?
	How do you, madam? How do you, my good lady?
DES.	Faith, half asleep. * * * * * * * * *
EM.	Good madam, what's the matter with my lord?
DES.	With who? * * * * * * * * * * *
EM.	Why, with my lord, madam. * * * * * * *
DES.	Who is thy lord? * * * * * * * * *
EM.	He that is yours, sweet lady.
DES.	I have none. Do not talk to me, Emilia;
	I cannot weep, nor answers have I none
	But what should go by water. Prithee, tonight
	Lay on my bed my wedding sheets – remember;
	And call thy husband hither.* * * * * * *
EM.	Here's a change indeed! * * * * * * * * (*Exit*)
DES.	'Tis meet I should be us'd so, very meet. . . . (IV ii 96–108)

I have marked incomplete lines with small asterisks; none of these lines has the ten syllables required to fill the pattern of an iambic pentameter. In this passage the text indicates how pauses could be sustained. At the start, Desdemona is 'half asleep': she does not know of whom Emilia speaks. Misunderstandings halt the talk until Desdemona asks a direct question. Then, as soon as she has said that she has no lord, she speedily seeks to stop further enquiry. The fourth line from the end – 'But what should go by water. Prithee, tonight' – could have two different metrical bases. With elision, it could be said without breaking the run of one verse-line; and so Desdemona's thoughts would seem to rush forward. But if no elision is permitted and a pause is taken at the full stop, the line could be read as two half-lines between which Desdemona does indeed weep or struggle against doing so. Desdemona's next unmistakable half-line shows that Emilia hesitates before she leaves on her errand. Then Emilia's concluding half-line shows that Desdemona is also silent before she speaks in soliloquy from the very depths of her being.

A useful way of exploring a text is to make a transcript which shows clearly all incomplete verse-lines, and then try to write in stage-directions that will account for the pauses that these indicate. It is an exercise that can lead on, with the help of the chessmen or other manikins described in chapter 5, to a fuller examination of stage activity that would alert a reader to the absence of precise or complete directions in authoritative texts.

First, all entries should be rewritten so that their order and manner of moving are prescribed; if clothes have been changed since the last appearance, these should be noted. Next, exits should be described with similar care, noting speed, order, direction, manner. Then stage-directions should be added for all the actions that are implied in the dialogue, such as kneeling, weeping, kissing or touching. Whenever the words of the text state or imply that the persons on stage alter their positions, or that a figure crosses from one group to another or walks about the stage, those actions should be given precise and detailed stage-directions. If more than one reader undertakes this exercise, various additions to the text can be compared and differences of opinion investigated further. It is instructive to consult several printed editions to see if the various editors have added directions of the same kind and in the same places. Photographic reproductions of early printed editions may also be consulted, especially where more than one authoritative text exists. (But too great reliance should not be given to these, because – as we have already noted – Elizabethan compositors often misplaced directions in order to fit them into the space available on their pages.) Obviously texts printed from the author's own manuscript have especially valuable directions; but these are sometimes very incomplete, especially with regard to exits.

There will be many places in a text where stage-directions can never be formulated with certainty or precision. This is why most editors supply as few as possible, and those in the simplest of forms. But a reader should not be misled by this tactful and almost inevitable conspiracy of silence: a great deal of imaginative, inventive and tentative creation of his own is required if the plays are not to flow past too easily in the mind, as words only, without regard for the living persons who speak them and who sustain them, or even counterstate them, by their actions.

Another passage in *Othello* will illustrate the need for this special vigilance with regard to stage-directions. In Act III, scene iii, most editions read more or less as follows:

OTH.	I have a pain upon my forehead here.
DES.	Faith, that's with watching; 'twill away again.
	Let me but bind it hard, within this hour
	It will be well. (*He puts the handkerchief from him, and she drops it*)
OTH.	Your napkin is too little.
	Let it alone. Come, I'll go in with you.
DES.	I am very sorry that you are not well. (*Exeunt*) (288–93)

The moment is so crucial to the play's development that every reader should be warned that the stage-direction in this printed text has no authority whatever. Neither Quarto nor Folio text has any direction at this point. Most editors supply something similar to the words quoted here, and so indicate that the loss of the handkerchief is Desdemona's fault; the New Arden editor follows Nicholas Rowe's text of 1709 with a simple '*She drops the handkerchief*'.

But Othello might be responsible for the accident. He might snatch it away from her and let it fall himself. Desdemona could have fastened the handkerchief securely before Othello tears it off and throws it onto the ground. Or he could react so violently that Desdemona could have no responsibility for the accident; this is implied in the Signet editor's stage-direction: '*He pushes the handkerchief away, and it falls.*' On the other hand, Desdemona might never have got the handkerchief to Othello's head, the sight of it being enough to arouse his irritation; she might drop it in astonishment or because she is instantly more concerned for her husband's well-being than for any token. Emilia, it is true, tells Iago that Desdemona 'Let it drop by negligence'; but we do not know if she is right about this or how truly she speaks; and her words do not explain how or why or at what moment. As we have seen, editors have interpreted Emilia's words in many different ways.

A further question must then arise: How do Desdemona and Othello leave the stage? Are they together, or does he leave at once so that she has to hurry after? The only certain fact about the stage-action here is that neither of them stops because the handkerchief has been dropped; perhaps everything happens so quickly that the audience itself does not realise that the handkerchief has been left on the ground, until Emilia picks it up. In this case, the whole incident could be much lighter than most editors imply, and the peace between Desdemona and Othello seem stronger than any conflict or uncertainty. 'Let it alone. Come, I'll go in with you' could indicate that for the moment the Moor's wife has 'sung the savageness out of a bear' (IV i 185–6).

This fatal moment in *Othello* illustrates what is true of every other moment in the plays: the words of the dialogue cannot tell us all, and printed stage-directions are always inadequate. Each text has to be imaginatively and responsibly explored in the light of a living performance of the drama.

☆

A reader's exploration of a play will move from words to action and then back again, and so the process will continue. A discovery on one front leads quickly to questions on the other, because the division between words and actions exists only in our minds. Ideally both enquiries are one, and in our more instinctive responses they do proceed inextricably.

So far in this book I have written most about the need to imagine the action of a play and to hear its words as part of a total performance, but I have no wish to undervalue the benefits of enquiring very closely into the meanings of words, their relationships, complexities and simplicities. I have been countering the tendency of many critics and almost all editors to limit their enquiry to *words*. While they ignore problems of punctuation and stage-directions, they retrieve meanings now lost in general usage and note multiple meanings, quotations from other writers, topical references, echoes from folk-lore and proverbs, and so on; they discuss fully every word that gives difficulty to a modern reader. All this can quicken our response to a text, but it is important to remember that the long and impressive notes of the Variorum or Arden editions have great limitations, even in their chosen semantic emphasis.

Even the limited task of annotating the words of a text cannot be done satisfactorily without envisaging the play in action. For example, only a few editors gloss Othello's opening words in the last scene: 'It is the cause, it is the cause, my soul' (v ii); and yet who can be sure what these words indicate about the great forces that are at full stretch within Othello? Is *the cause* an agent (perhaps in a bad sense), or the end (as in the 'final cause'), or the ground for action? Or is Othello referring to legal usage, whereby *the cause* signifies the subject for dispute or, even, the accusation? It is just possible that here, as elsewhere, Shakespeare alludes to a late Latin usage, where *cause* means disease or 'that which has to be cured'.

Once a reader replaces the conventional questions of an editor, 'What are the difficulties in this passage, and what can the words mean?', with the theatrical question, 'Why does this person in the drama say this word at this moment?', the fullest page of annotations may become insufficient. In Othello's 'It is the cause, it is the cause . . .', we should ask: Why *It* and not 'This' or 'She'? Why *is* and not 'was'? Why the repetition? (Obviously this question goes beyond the meaning of words.) And what force does *soul* have here for Othello, and at this point in the play? All these questions are important for the actor of the part, and so they should be explored.

Can Othello be remembering 'O my soul's joy', the cry with which he greeted Desdemona upon their reunion in Cyprus (II i 182)?; or his later realisation:

```
        . . .              Perdition catch my soul
     But I do love thee; and when I love thee not
     Chaos is come again.                          ?      (III iii 91–3)
```

Does *soul* mean the principle of life in Othello, his eternal being, or does it refer to the seat of his emotions? Of these two earlier passages, that in

Act II suggests the first sense, the other the second. Moreover, we should notice that, 50 lines after the opening words of Act v, scene ii, Othello calls Desdemona 'sweet soul': is it possible that *my soul*, in the context of 'it is the cause, my soul', is also a term of endearment for Desdemona? (The very expression is used in *Twelfth Night*, I v 253, in this manner – 'And call upon my soul within the house' – and in *A Midsummer Night's Dream* and *Cymbeline*.)

The questions raised by any line of text are far-reaching and delicate. In one way, obviously difficult words are the easiest to understand: a solution often clicks into place. Besides, we know that Shakespeare, in common with many contemporary writers, did coin new words and usages consciously, so that they would give pleasure as their meanings were recognised. (Bardolph's high-toned use of *accommodate*, when he is trying to impress Justice Shallow in *2 Henry IV*, III ii 65–6, is a comical demonstration of this skill.) But Shakespeare's use of idiomatic words and phrases that are sometimes very simple to read, his echoing of proverbs, variations of normal grammatical usage and small modifications proper to a special trade, profession, culture, age-group, sex, social class or intimate relationship – these are all more difficult to perceive and trace. Constant vigilance is needed, and an essentially theatrical enquiry.

A student is often faced with two or more possible meanings – sometimes with contrary meanings. This is part of the richness of Shakespeare's dialogue. If more than one interpretation of a word fits the context, all may be valid. Such ambiguities and double meanings are common in Elizabethan poetry and drama, and in the humour of all ages. They express minds in high excitement or deep involvement; and what may seem over-ingenious in explanation can be entirely lifelike in performance, as a natural overflow of sensation. The test must be whether complexity of meaning is appropriate to our sense of the dramatic moment for the person who is speaking.

A wider range of possible meanings than those quoted in any edition is easily discovered if the reader has access to two important publications. The first is the Oxford *New English Dictionary* (volumes published between 1888 and 1933) which enumerates and exemplifies all the meanings that its numerous compilers had recognised in books of the period. The second is a Shakespeare concordance. Computers are now producing replacements for John Bartlett's *Complete Concordance*, first published in 1894, but for most readers of Shakespeare this late-Victorian work is more than adequate and not prohibitively expensive. Each citation is quoted at sufficient length to awaken a memory of its context. A reader should be warned, however, than Bartlett is really two concordances, the poems and sonnets having their own lists at the back of the volume. I find it hard to say which of these two publications is the

more useful for an independent exploration of Shakespeare's text: the
New English Dictionary can suggest meanings for any word, and the
Concordance can reveal if any of these corresponds with Shakespeare's
usage elsewhere in his works.

These two reference books should be sought out first, and then
additions can be made to the student's resources. In 'Suggestions for
Further Reading' at the end of the book I list works of great usefulness in
such areas as historical grammar, pronunciation, language-style and
rhetoric.

For the reader who has limited access to libraries and limited time,
the best book to purchase as a supplement to Shakespeare's text is
undoubtedly C. T. Onions's *A Shakespeare Glossary* (final revision 1953).
Professor Onions was one of the editors of the *New English Dictionary* and
in this small volume devoted to Shakespeare he has supplied

. . . definitions and illustrations of words or senses of words now obsolete or
surviving only in provincial or archaic use, together with explanations of others
involving allusions not generally familiar, and of proper names carrying with
them some connotative signification or offering special interest or difficulty in
the passages in which they occur.   (*Preface*)

Of course, the dangers of using this *Glossary* are that it is selective and that
it does not list modern usages which were current – sometimes
surprisingly – in the sixteenth and early seventeenth centuries. But it
contains much to awaken appreciation of Shakespeare's text and to
recover what the passage of time has obscured.

8 | *Speech*

Scholastic debates about the meanings of words, like our consideration of *cause, soul* and *accommodate* in the previous chapter, seem a far cry from the experience of plays in performance. In one important sense they are: an actor's language is alive and not dead; and the moment of speech has no leisure for compromise or indecision. We do not go to the theatre to recognise the meanings of words; we react to performances, to total embodiments of a play's text.

But, in another sense, scholarly commentaries and footnotes do contribute to the performance of a play. The actors have considered and used whatever can be discovered about the words, as part of a process in which they have drawn on many other perceptions of quite different kinds and at various levels of consciousness. The study of dead words on a page is one element in a very complex creative adventure which can be charted step by step. It is the finished performance which can never be satisfactorily described; not even the spoken words are able to provide an adequate paraphrase for that. Yet in the brilliant clarity of a deeply considered and fully achieved performance, the lost meanings traced in scholarly annotation are reborn, and multiple meanings are able to live together. Then Shakespeare's text is seen, felt and experienced, as well as heard; and all kinds of scholarship fall into their appropriate and secondary positions.

All speech, on stage and off, is difficult to explain, and so there is no reason to view lengthy and inconclusive annotations with suspicion. Nor should we wish that Shakespeare's 'difficult' words could be replaced by simpler, everyday ones which an audience would recognise instantly: that would introduce new obscurities of meaning, besides destroying the metrical form, rhythms and texture of the original. In the 1960s, the National Theatre in London tried to do this, and hired the poet Robert Graves to make substitutions in the text of *Much Ado About Nothing*; but by the time the actors had worked their way through to the opening performance, almost all the simplifications had been replaced by the supposedly harder words of the original. Almost nothing had been gained by removing the obvious difficulties. The director should have known better: an audience responds to an image of life and not to a collection of words. In the bright mirror of the lifelike stage, very individual and complex experiences may be seen with the deep shock of instant recognition.

The more we value performance, the more we must study the text. It is the only permanent element in Shakespeare's plays and our sole means of contact with his creative mind. We must learn as much as we can about the words and how they interact with each other; and then we must find how to speak those words and also – and this is much more difficult – how to *act* the words. In this process the most complicated speech may come to have a single, overwhelming and apparently simple effect, or the most ordinary words leave disquieting echoes. An audience may scarcely hear some words, even though they have been carefully studied and clearly spoken, because the play has moved outside the range of ordinary recognitions.

Sometimes the text itself reminds us of the great difference between performance and literary study. When Othello says 'Pray you chuck, come hither. . . . Let me see your eyes; look in my face' (IV ii 25–7), a literary student might note the unusual intimacy of *chuck* and the formality of the following requests, and so predict a careful, quiet episode. But Desdemona's comment – 'What horrible fancy's this?' – must alert him to the fact that Othello's speeches are frightening and almost crazed in performance. His next words are coarse and overbearing, but Desdemona hears more than that:

> Upon my knees, what doth your speech import?
> I understand a fury in your words,
> But not the words.

Such descriptions of the effect of a performance are rare, and Shakespeare's usual method is to rely on the words themselves to lead the actor to an appropriate dynamic for each speech. A reader should learn to recognise and interpret the various clues to performance that lie within the text, the outward signs of inner energy of thought and feeling. An actor should guide his whole performance by them.

Between the printed text and actual performance are interposed a great many skills both of study and performance. Some readers and actors respond very easily to the demands of metre and the varying sounds or colours of words, and so they speak a text with lively authority. But this touches only the surface of a play, and an actor who reads well 'off the page' may sometimes fail to progress further towards a fully realised performance. So seductive are the immediate rewards of speaking Shakespeare's words that the actor can remain a 'talking head', and never attain the further ability to seek out and represent the thought-processes, feelings and personal life which Shakespeare imagined in composition and which underly the words of his text.

Besides studying sense and metre, the actor must discover the drive behind the words: that which makes him say those words and no others. In order to re-create the inner force he must train himself to make quick changes, from moment to moment, and to reach deep within his own being. Othello's first appearance calls for just this skill. His first sustained speech reads:*

> Let him do his spite.
> My services which I have done the signiory
> Shall out-tongue his complaints. 'Tis yet to know –
> Which, when I know that boasting is an honour,
> I shall promulgate – I fetch my life and being
> From men of royal siege and my demerits
> May speak unbonneted to as proud a fortune
> As this that I have reach'd. For know Iago,
> But that I love the gentle Desdemona,
> I would not my unhoused free condition
> Put into circumscription and confine
> For the seas' worth.   ...   (i ii 17–28)

After his first short rebuttal of Brabantio's 'spite', Othello settles into thoughts that he has had before, and now expresses an easy generality about 'My services', sharpened by the brief sarcasm of 'out-tongue' at the expense of his father-in-law. Then his mind looks further afield and backwards in time, but hesitates about making his thought public – 'Tis yet to know' – and plays with the ornate 'I shall promulgate' in juxtaposition to the direct 'I fetch'. This double consciousness continues: he is half-playful in 'unbonneted', as if encouraged by confidence in his new marriage, and then reticent in the direct simplicity of 'this that I have reach'd'. Although a delicate parenthesis has been sustained within a thought that is continued for five lines, it is here that the speech buckles suddenly. 'For know Iago' breaks the rhythm and is the first indication of a new intention. Then the new message starts with another subsidiary clause – 'But that I love the gentle Desdemona' – which is the first thought in the whole speech to

---

* From this quotation forward, I simplify the punctuation of Peter Alexander's edition, relying chiefly on full stops. Readers are referred to page 85 above for an explanation of this procedure.

run without pause the length of one verse-line and to be completed within it. Its words are far simpler than all the earlier ones, except the very brief and decisive 'Let him do his spite' and 'For know Iago'. New, too, is the word 'Desdemona'. With a great deal of expository cunning, Shakespeare has avoided using her name throughout the preceding scene which was all to do with telling Brabantio that Desdemona has eloped. Now she is named with the epithet 'gentle', both tender and civilised. The verb in this preparatory clause is the monosyllabic 'love'. Perhaps no other simple-sounding word can touch consciousness so deeply and so individually; in a thoughtful context, it is one of the most demanding words that any actor has to speak. Only careful imaginative exploration, a full identification with the part at a profound level of consciousness, will enable this word to ring true and deep in a believable performance. Then, after being held back by this unforced, unrushed and wonderfully uncomplicated line, Othello's main thought of proud independence continues, sustained by the idea of 'the seas' worth', an image at once grand and perilous, words to which a man of Othello's experience would bring exact meaning.

In such a speech the actor will gain attention by speaking the words clearly and with 'good discretion'. But if he wishes to draw on their full strength, he has two further steps to take. Both his mind and being must respond to the words' meanings, allusions and references; and both mind and being must move within the strict time and proportion of their syntax and structure. The second process is, perhaps, the more difficult: the actor must seek out the inner processes that put each of the words in its place, so that his imagination and performance represent the complex shape of the speech, as well as its verbal richness; then he must act so that all is as life-like as breathing, and as necessary.

A short speech from the same scene shows how the text may demand a powerful and extraordinary effect by the shape and structure of a single line. A body of fully armed men are urged forward by the alarmed Brabantio and confront Othello, outnumbering his attendants:

CAS.	Here comes another troop to seek for you.
IAGO.	It is Brabantio. General, be advis'd
	He comes to bad intent.
OTH.	Holla. Stand there.
ROD.	Signior, it is the Moor.
BRA.	Down with him, thief.
IAGO.	You, Roderigo. Come sir, I am for you.
OTH.	Keep up your bright swords for the dew will rust them. . . .

(I ii 54–9)

The stage has filled quickly with urgent movement, drawn swords and lights. Othello's quick order is disregarded and on 'thief' there is further action and noise. Then Othello's single sustained line quells the violence. He has just come from Desdemona and so he is likely to be unarmed, but all the enraged and alarmed men obey him. He is at the height of his powers as a leader and in full confidence of his new love. Edmund Kean's performance at this moment caught the imagination of John Keats:

. . . his throat had commanded where swords were as thick as reeds. From eternal risk, he speaks as though his body were unassailable.[1]

Othello then turns to Brabantio with respect and something of the dispassionate humour with which he had spoken of him in his absence:

> Good Signior you shall more command with years
> Than with your weapons.

The half-line is not completed; for a moment even Brabantio is silent.

In this first scene, the dynamics of Othello's speeches present the Moor of Venice as a man strong enough to act with great economy. His power and passions are both evident – likewise his intelligence and physical prowess, his outward assurance and inner sense of danger. He knows both violence and peace.

The words of Shakespeare's text must not be studied apart from their performance. At first this seems a forbidding requirement to lay upon a reader of the text, because only an actor's imagination seems able to reach down to its roots and find the hidden life. But an actor will also feel at a disadvantage. He knows that a lifetime well spent in the pursuit of his profession is a necessary preparation for any of Shakespeare's great roles.

Besides, the interconnections between the various parts of his task are complicated and mostly unconscious. (That is why theatre schools separate the teaching of 'Speech' from the teaching of 'Acting' and 'Movement', and usually treat 'Dramatic Literature' as yet another independent subject.) Almost always the discovery of an appropriate performance for any line of text seems, in the last resort, to be fortuitous. Both actor and reader need imagination, experience, open-mindedness and luck; and both must be perpetual students. This way they will find that encouragement comes quickly, because a summit always keeps reappearing to view.

The reader must begin by recognising the range of an actor's attention and then follow where this understanding leads.

☆

Anyone who wants to understand what a speech can do in a play must be prepared to speak aloud. This is not the same thing as acting, but it can achieve much more than theory or description. Something of what happens within the lines, on them and around them, can be experienced by using one's own voice; the clues to performance that lie within the text will become more recognisable.

Many readers will be shy of speech and prefer to listen to recordings of the plays. But this does not achieve the same ends. Most recordings are made by practised actors and present the effect of one particular reading. They are useful to students who find that reading a text silently is difficult, but they do not reveal the hidden multitude of signs whereby Shakespeare has 'directed' his own plays. A listener may enjoy the actors' rendering of a text, but he will not learn to read and seek out its dramatic life independently. Moreover, recordings are made by actors standing still or sitting in a studio and are thus disembodied in a double sense; in true performance, speech is at one with action, for actors and audience. The more skilful the sound-recording, the more it bypasses essential questions. The best use of these aids to study and enjoyment is to have two or three different versions of the same play and compare them, scene by scene and speech by speech: then, as the actors' individual contributions and decisions are distinguished, useful questions will arise.

A better way of discovery is simple and brutal: shut yourself away and read a whole play aloud. Something of the weight and length of the play will register: its continuous demand upon the wits of the actors; moments when a speaker must stop and unravel a long sentence before he can make any kind of sense; moments when progress is suddenly easy or when speech seems to glide over great and complicated happenings. These elementary, first-hand perceptions are worth far more than the pleasures of responding to a sound recording made by practised actors, and can be just as enjoyable.

Having begun to read aloud, the next step is to read very short passages very carefully. Try taking only a few lines and speaking them in different ways. Do not attempt to 'act' them, but alter tempo, pitch, volume, phrasing, stress or point. A pause should be taken between each experiment, to allow the new reading to register clearly in the mind. A tape recorder can store up the more interesting results – and the almost meaningless may be among these – so that they may be played back on another occasion and judged more objectively.

In *Othello*, Iago's second long speech to Roderigo could provide several different opportunities for such experiments. Here is the beginning:

> I follow him to serve my turn upon him.
> We cannot all be masters, nor all masters
> Cannot be truly follow'd. . . .   (I i 42–4)

For a start, use the first line only. Speak it fast and note its effect. Then speak it as slowly as possible, pronouncing each word distinctly, almost separately; and again stop to notice the new effect. Next, vary the volume using a moderate speed, first very loud and then very quietly; probably you will be able to go further in each direction than on your first attempts. Then pitch should be changed, using moderate speed and volume; and again you will be able to make a greater variation on a second or third trial. You are now in a position to combine the various readings in different ways: quiet, fast and low-pitched; quiet, fast and high; quiet, slow and high; and so on. Some combinations are virtually impossible, such as loud, slow and high; but even these oddities can help to establish the range of effects that are practicable.

By this time the reader's mind will be full of many impressions and almost certainly very muddled. A pause is needed to take stock of what has happened; and then the reader can move on to another part of the speech or, using the same fragment, he can attempt more subtle vocal changes. Speed, volume and pitch can be changed within the line and in various ways; but probably the most useful experiment at this stage is to vary pointing and phrasing. Using a moderate speed and level delivery, try speaking the line in one phrase and then in two: 'I follow him to serve my turn upon him' and 'I follow him // to serve my turn upon him'. Volume, pitch and tempo can be varied for the two halves, with or without a slight pause between them. Now more of the text should be introduced and phrasing varied over the longer reading. The next line and a half can be tried with no pause, and then with two:

> We cannot all be masters//nor all masters
> Cannot be truly follow'd.

It can follow quickly on the previous line, or after a considerable pause. Speed, volume and pitch can also be varied in these different renderings and between the separated phrases.

The next experiment is to choose different words for stress:

> I *follow him* to serve *my turn* upon him.
> I follow *him* to *serve* my turn upon *him*.
> I *follow* him to serve *my turn* upon him.
> I *follow* him to *serve* my turn upon *him*.

The next line and a half will offer other choices, so that the reader can stress variously *We, cannot, all, masters, truly* or *follow'd*. The repetitions can be stressed equally – *cannot, all* and *masters* – or only the first occurence of each word so that other words will lift into prominence when they are repeated; or only the second occurence can be stressed, in which case the sentence will slow up progressively. What is interesting, and a main purpose behind speaking aloud, is that these technically varied utterances, with no attempt to act or portray a character, will suggest varied consciousnesses behind the words and sustaining them. These explorations are very elementary and yet they can be very bewildering. They should be taken slowly and in small doses. Soon a reader will become more deft at speaking and quicker at distinguishing effects, and so he will be ready for longer passages and possibly for further variations of voice including changes of enunciation, texture and colour. These last alterations are particularly interesting to apply to descriptive passages, like Iago's 'Many a duteous and knee-crooking knave' in the same speech, and to simply worded ones, like his concluding 'I am not what I am'. Until a reader is relatively practised in speaking aloud in this experimental way, I think three or four lines are about as much as can be handled at any one time.

By then another technical experiment should be undertaken: speaking with careful attention to metre. The staple of almost all Shakespearean verse is the iambic pentameter: a line that can be counted in ten syllables, alternately light and heavy, or unstressed and stressed. It can be divided into five feet, each of two syllables. Few of Shakespeare's lines are completely regular, and even those will vary one from the other because all the alternating syllables cannot be equally stressed or equally unstressed. But the iambic pentameter is the norm underlying the many variations, and it is this norm that provides the ongoing beat: a sustaining power, a sense of expectation and continuity, of energy, freedom, fulfilment. The incomplete or half-lines, which we have already noticed, interrupt this norm, and thereby gain considerable dramatic force; Shakespeare used them as clear stage-directions, indicating pauses for action, reflection or contrary impulses. When two speakers share a line of verse or when a new sentence begins in mid-line, the fulfilment of the norm gives an impression of ongoing energy or direct interaction.

The same passages can be used for speaking with strict attention to metre:

> I fóllow hím to sérve my túrn upon hím.
> We cánnot áll be másters nór all másters
> Cannót be trúly fóllow'd. Yóu shall márk

There are only two necessary irregularities in the verse here, and both are dramatically useful. In the first line, *upon* has to be a single unstressed syllable: this has the effect of giving more energy to *him*, a naturally light sound, so that the line finishes clearly. In the second line, the concluding *masters* has an additional unstressed syllable – this is called a feminine ending – which tends to make the regularity of the

beginning of the next line sound like a regaining of strength and balance. For this reason, I think that the unusual stress on the second syllable of *Cannot* in the third line is probably not appropriate; this line should begin with a reversal of normal stressing. This is a very common variation of the iambic norm which gives a quickening effect that is especially useful when sense and syntax follow without break from one line into another.

Speaking these three lines with five equally strong stresses in each would produce a very heavy effect. Usually three stressed syllables are the main emphases in any one line, sometimes only two and sometimes four. In this a reader has to choose between several options. I would give only one rule for guidance: the fourth syllable – the second strong stress – is almost always regular. It is the most effective anchor to the hidden norm; when this holds, a greater flexibility is possible elsewhere. So our three lines might be read:

> I fóllow hím to sérve my túrn upon hím.
> We cánnot áll be masters nor all másters
> Cannot be trúly fóllow'd. You shall márk   . . .

In these experiments with the metre of a few lines out of context, many modifications can be made quickly and easily, but this would not be so in true rehearsal and performance. Such changes are intimately concerned with the life-likeness of performance and with the flow and vitality of each scene. Perhaps the last line of this speech will show how deep the matter goes:

> But I will wear my heart upon my sleeve
> For daws to peck at. I am not what I am.

The last six words are the problem here. The penultimate line has three or four regular stresses: on *wear*, *heart* and *sleeve*, and perhaps on *I*. The last line has two clear stresses, at the beginning, on *daws* and *peck*, which leaves a maximum of three to share between the last six syllables and words – for each word is a monosyllable. After the unstressed *at*, the first *I* must take a stress, which leaves regular stresses on *not* and the second *I*. But then the two verbs, which are of crucial importance to the meaning of the sentence, are both unstressed, the second seeming to be a feminine ending which Iago has no means of strengthening by further speech. The only recourse within the measure of a single line would be to stress the words thus:

> For dáws to péck at. Í am nót what I ám.

This would be both clumsy and heavy, and not at all easy to pronounce clearly. Probably the best solution would be to leave 'For daws to peck at.' as an incomplete verse-line to be followed by a pause in which Iago may move away from Roderigo to smile or laugh, or in which he can watch Roderigo or turn to the audience. 'I am not what I am' would then be spread out, as another incomplete and tauntingly irregular line: 'I am nót whát I ám' or 'Í am nót what Í ám', or 'I ám nót what Í ám'. Possibly each word could be stressed with the freedom of prose, or five clear and distinct stresses chosen. The sentence could be spoken very quickly. Certainly Roderigo's next line is not a continuation either in sense or metre: it starts with a new thought and a new rhythm:

> Whát a full fórtune does the thíck-lips ówe
> If hé can cárry't thús.

Roderigo may not have heard Iago's 'I am not what I am'.

For all the basic simplicity of the iambic pentameter, an investigation of the metrical element of Shakespeare's text leads to most complicated issues. Sometimes the implied stage-direction is unequivocal – for instance three consecutive stressed syllables can almost never be correct – but more often a temporary resolution of problems must wait for a full performance of the play.

As Shakespeare's career proceeded, his handling of metre became more and more subtle, more closely involved with the movement of thought and the state of being behind the spoken words. If we wish to understand his practice, the best course is to start with early plays and so approach the problems of *Othello* and other major works by the same route as that taken by Shakespeare and the actors of the Chamberlain's and the King's Men.

For example, the early plays show clearly how verse-lining is related to syntax and phrasing. Much of the on-going energy of the dialogue derives from Shakespeare's handling of these interconnections. Here is Richard of Gloucester from *King Henry VI, Part Three*:

> And yet I know not how to get the crown
> For many lives stand between me and home
> And I – like one lost in a thorny wood
> That rents the thorns and is rent with the thorns,
> Seeking a way and straying from the way
> Not knowing how to find the open air
> But toiling desperately to find it out –
> Torment myself to catch the English crown
> And from that torment I will free myself
> Or hew my way out with a bloody axe.   . . .   (III ii 172–81)

The units of thought and expression march fairly within the measure of the lines. The one essential break in sense comes in the third line where the series of parenthetical similes begins after only two syllables. The antithetical thoughts of the third and fourth lines fit tightly within the pentameters, but with neat variation of stress in their second halves. Then the third double thought takes up two lines, and so brings the parenthetical series to a firm end. From its eight-syllable start in the third line to this conclusion, an impression is given of Richard's exploratory thought elbowing its way forward, impelled by a strengthening feeling of frustration. In contrast, the main clause of the next long sentence starts strongly with tight phrasing and a reversed first foot supplying the crux of the whole paragraph:

> Tórment mysélf to cátch the Énglish crówn.

The next thought starts more lightly, but the fourth syllable is a repeat of *tor*ment and then the line rises to the regular ending in 'frée mysélf' which repeats *myself* and so emphasises the potent verb *free*: a monosyllable which counterstates all the similes of the parenthesis. This is also the first line that does not require a natural pause at the end: sense and rhythm move straight on to the concluding line, with a strong stress on *hew* and another firm regular ending on *blóody áxe*, made all the more impressive by the reversed third foot, 'óut with':

> And from that tórment Í will frée mysélf
> Or héw my wáy óut with a blóody áxe.

A purely technical exploration of Shakespeare's dialogue may go so far. Already a definite, continuous consciousness has been suggested for the speaker: his actions have also begun to come into play, and his state of being. Further study would involve still deeper responses to the text, and the discovery and development of a complete performance. Here a reader is at a disadvantage in comparison with an actor in rehearsal and performance: a full committal, expertise and long experience are all needed, as well as curiosity and imagination, and the interplay between one actor and the others. No short cuts are available. But the actor has his disadvantages too. His own instincts, his director and his audience will encourage him to simplify the performance he gives in order for it to become more effective. Usually this is at the cost of the wit, vitality and variety of feeling that he senses within the play, waiting for release and re-creation.

A very simple – albeit taxing and slow-moving – exercise can give some impression of what may be involved in the actor's work. A single

line, or possibly two lines, should be memorised. Let us take 'Keep up
your bright swords for the dew will rust them', which has already been
considered in its dramatic setting at pages 95–6 above.

Now sit relaxed in some quiet, neutral and familiar room, and start
speaking the line, almost silently and without particular emphasis, some
ten or twenty times. During this stage of the exercise think of the words
in print, and then the sound of each voiced letter or letters. Now stop
and, closing your eyes, picture to yourself any sword that you have seen
and can remember; imagine that you are grasping it, feeling its weight,
and then holding it forward as if to challenge someone who is similarly
armed. Try to visualise the sword precisely, from its handle and
ornamentation to the blade's edge and furthermost tip. If possible, say
quite quietly, 'sword': allow the sound to suit the imagined picture, the
picture the sound. Next visualise more swords – if possible many more
swords, but each one imagined separately. Perhaps knives and axes, or
other offensive weapons with cutting edges, are more easily envisaged; if
so, use them. Slowly, and with precise detail, visualise these weapons
held out in challenge and attack; and say that word 'swords' again – or,
rather, let the word come out in response to your imagination. Try to
half-listen to yourself saying the word, experimenting with the picture
in your mind and with the sound, and when the word sounds
unexpectedly true to the changing image remember both the sound and
that momentary image. 'Bright' is the next word to try; first by itself,
and then in association with naked steel in a sharp dawn light. By this
time 'your' has to be imagined too: those who hold the swords, the
soldiers following Othello and Cassio, and the larger group of
Brabantio's followers who are all excited and energised by the chase
through the narrow streets of Venice. It is hard to visualise an historical
Venice or London; some paintings can help, and so can films. But it is
probably best to feed into your imaginary picture some film-shots of
street violence that you have seen on television, or some moments of
violence from your own experience. Let other senses come into play:
sound, smell, taste, physical pain. Now it is time to say 'your bright
swords', changing both image and utterance until the spoken words
seem truest to the imagined reality.

A break from the concentrated work is necessary now. Sit back and
open your eyes and let what ever will come into the mind; take a cup of
coffee, talk if you are in company – for this exercise is good to do with
another person, one giving instructions for changing and developing the
mental image and the other responding by speaking the words. The
next stage must be 'Keep up': this can be said as a detached order in any
real situation, possibly on a parade ground if you have actual
experience of military drill, or in a gymnasium during some competitive
event or training session. Then the whole of the first part of the line can

be spoken very slowly, waiting to recreate a precise mental image before speaking each separated word: 'Keep . . . up . . . your . . . bright . . . swords'. If you can create an image of being surrounded by many armed men, so much the better; but in any case, be sure to create a precise image of dawn light on naked blades, or at least on one very particular and actual sword-blade. Repeat the half-line several times, pausing when necessary to envisage all the action and then all the situation and setting. Realise how one and then another sword might move. Say 'Keep up' as in necessary haste, and then again in calm determination so that everyone can hear and be reassured. Then say the whole phrase again, remembering all that you have already associated with 'bright' and 'swords'.

Again a pause is needed, in which you should move or speak with someone else. Then become once more fully aware of yourself sitting in the room and say the phrase again, using whatever seems the most precise and helpful instigations for your imagination – 'Keep up your bright swords' – but this time go on and add 'for the dew will rust them'. The next step involves the same slow, step-by-step process for the second half of the line. Isolate 'dew' first of all, and create pictures in your mind of dew wherever you have experienced it. Let a particular place where you have seen, touched and perhaps tasted it come into your mind so that your sensuous and precisely visual memories of the morning sky, blades of grass or someone's close presence are all recalled. From time to time, say 'dew' slowly. Let the sound of the word respond to your thoughts in any way, speaking slowly, quickly, lightly, however seems best to you. Repeat the word as you fasten precisely on different memories. Then work in the same way on 'rust', and 'will rust them'. When your reaction to each word is secure – that is, when you have selected the memories and sounds which seem most potent for each part of the line – you are ready to speak the whole line.

The connective word 'for' has not been prepared, and if the speaker's mind is still functioning with a whole sequence of imaginary images it will be difficult to say. A major problem has come into focus. Are the fresh coldness of 'dew' and the waste and ineffectualness of 'rust' the dominant ideas which motivate the whole verse-line and so provide the impulse to speak? Or is a response to 'bright swords' a first, self-contained instinct and the second, giving the motive for speech, a familiar instinct to command with the brief and efficient 'Keep up'? Or to put this question in another form, is the single sentence and verse-line one thought-action, or is it two? Both ways of motivating the line can be attempted, very slowly at first, and the results tape-recorded for subsequent comparison. By this time the speaker is on the verge of acting, and so the dramatic situation must be brought to mind too, and the actual body, mentality and sense-experience of Othello as he has just left his new bride to face this crisis of command. My own view is that the line is one action, possibly spoken as a single phrase, and that it represents the experienced fighter and new husband confronting the energetic excitement of younger men. But further possibilities should also be considered. Perhaps the common Shakespearean pun on *due* and *dew* is present here; if so, my preference for the single motivation of the line would be strengthened and the progression to his next words made more explicable and more effective, for Brabantio represents law, order and responsibility. Moreover, by starting from the idea of *dew*, a certain gentleness, delicacy and openness to sensual experience can be transmitted, which would be entirely suitable to an Othello who comes from his 'gentle love' who has committed herself, at this very moment, to live with him. Perhaps he commands so completely because his authority has a sense of peace that is new and surprising to others and grounded deep within him. The alternative performance of the line is sharp, mocking and egotistical, drawing on customary authority and given edge by Othello's new personal experience. Some actors may prefer this, despite the fact that a single response sustained throughout the whole sentence can be strong without having to be loud, as compared with a two-stage reaction involving a break in delivery of the verse-line.

The slow vocal exercise is now at its end. Only real rehearsal and performance with a full cast of gifted actors engaged in the whole play could go much further in exploration and discovery. But the elementary trail will have served its purpose if it has shown that a study of Shakespeare's text involves the study of speech and that this is an exploratory, precise and open engagement which needs time, quiet concentration, patience, quickness of intelligence, personal and physical imagination, and total commitment, if it is to be effective.

9 | *Motivation and Subtext*

By speaking the lines aloud and by attending performances and rehearsals, a student begins to understand how a text comes alive in speech, action and performance. He will also learn to recognise the cues which Shakespeare has written into his dialogue to guide an actor and control dramatic effect. Meaning, allusion, reference, repetition, double meanings, syntax, metre, verse-lining, rhetorical structure, exchange of lead, interruption, silence, description of speech or action are among the obvious cues we have noticed already. Others are more hidden, and a reader, like an actor, has to be aware of them.

Although everyone will pay attention to syntax, it is one of the most undervalued guides to performance. Actors tend to work from phrase to phrase, giving meaning, colour and emphasis according to each word or phrase as it is spoken. Such performances live through the words at the moment of utterance, and they can easily become fragmentary and shallow because the long-term effects of grammatical structure are not utilised.

Both actor and reader should study syntax to discover the motive for speech: its origin, the point from which true energy springs. Usually this can be found in the main verb, or main predicate, of each sentence, whether that unit is short and simple, or long and complicated. Almost all the details of a speech depend upon this active source.

For example, Desdemona addresses the Senate in *Othello*:

> That I did love the Moor to live with him,
> My downright violence and storm of fortunes
> May trumpet to the world. My heart's subdu'd
> Even to the very quality of my lord.
> I saw Othello's visage in his mind
> And to his honours and his valiant parts
> Did I my soul and fortunes consecrate.
> So that, dear lords, if I be left behind,
> A moth of peace, and he go to the war,
> The rites for Why I love him are bereft me
> And I a heavy interim shall support
> By his dear absence. Let me go with him.　　　(I iii 248–59)

Although her first words are about 'love', these are sustained by the verb 'trumpet' in the third line and dependent upon it; and that idea is also related to 'violence' and 'storm'. So the beginning of her speech is not gentle, reasonable or personal, as the tenderness of its first words might suggest if spoken by themselves, or if the first line were rephrased as a separate sentence. Desdemona starts speaking because she is aware of her own strength, independence, openness and deep, dangerous passion. She is also very much in control, because 'did love' is linked quickly, firmly and even wittily with 'to live'. In contrast, the force of the next sentence lies in 'subdu'd'; a new self-revealing and self-denying motivation, placed very early in the word-order, close to the subject of the sentence, 'My heart'. Desdemona now speaks without hesitation or preparation, and also without over-emphasis because she is able to fill out the new idea in the unforced fourth line, with its pun on 'quality', meaning the soldierly profession that takes Othello away from Venice and also his natural gifts of good nature.

The next sentence changes tense and therefore its basic attitude. Moreover its verb comes immediately after the singular personal pronoun, 'I saw'. Desdemona now gives evidence directly, although she is speaking of highly sensitive, intimate moral and social issues. With no sign of conflict or hesitation, she passes on, with a simple 'And', to speak of Othello as a great general and holds back the verb to the very end of the further line. That motivating centre of the sentence is 'consecrate' and it is separated by almost a whole line from its subject, 'I'; it is also emphasised by the preparatory 'Did' at the beginning of the second line. At this stage of her address to the Senate, Desdemona is personally direct, formal, firm, delicate, unhurried and bold: 'I saw . . . Did I . . . consecrate'. Both her 'soul' and 'fortunes', her hopes of joy in this life and for ever, together with Othello's 'honours' and his brave, strong, physical body are held together by whatever force Desdemona finds in, or gives to, 'consecrate'. That sustaining idea – however dangerously idealised, passionately intense, or childishly confident it may be– controls and colours every other word in the sentence.

At the end of a line and sentence, climactically placed and in charge of divergent thoughts, 'consecrate' is the very heart of Desdemona's appeal. Her next words are simple, but the syntax is quickly complicated. She begins with 'So that . . . if I', but carefully interpolates 'dear lords' which is a more assured and direct appeal that breaks through the expression of her own concerns. 'A moth of peace' is a new phrase or idea, and a delicately imaginative one, that interrupts the main line of thought in the 'if' clause. The subject of the new sentence does not come until 'The rites'; and its verb arrives still later, near the end of the line, with 'are bereft me'. In contrast with her first strong appeal, she is now revealing the fragility and quick, varied impulses of her present condition. A further, more resolute sentence begins with 'And' and is sustained by 'shall support' – again a new tense and therefore a new mental engagement. But this time, the verb is neither at the end nor the beginning; it is followed by a subsidiary phrase, 'By his dear absence', which starts a new verse-line and may be expressed without any contrary colouring from the preceding verb. Perhaps she has come close to tears, with 'bereft' and 'heavy', and now, in a kind of afterthought or release of previously hidden thoughts, his absence fills her mind completely. That would explain the change of syntax, tense and style for the next five words that conclude her speech, 'Let me go with him'. As an independent syntactical unit and as a sequence of almost colourless, open words, this last sentence starts after a brief break in the sense and perhaps a quick breath between sentences. The simple words can speak according to Desdemona's inner sense of her situation as that has developed while she has been speaking. The faces that she looks at may tell her that she has won her appeal, or she may see that she has no true support besides Othello. Or, more simply, she has said all that can be said publicly, and so speaks now with a renewed reserve before her passions repossess her mind in silence.

The length of each sentence or complete thought, and the position and nature of the main verb within each sentence, are crucial stage-directions to actor or reader. In the line 'Keep up your bright swords for the dew will rust them', discussed in the last chapter, the syntax was ambiguous. The main verb 'Keep up' could speak for itself and the final phrase 'for the dew will rust them' be a new and separate thought; but there is another energising verb in that concluding phrase, and so the ideas associated with 'dew' might have registered early in Othello's mind and 'Keep up' imply a half-conscious desire to save the fresh dew (and due) of his love from any disturbance. In much the same way, 'support' in Desdemona's speech could be motivated and coloured by 'his dear absence', although that phrase, lacking a verb, is not such an active one. Besides 'Let me go with him', that follows immediately, is unambiguous and free to speak for itself, except as it arises out of the whole foregoing speech and Desdemona's response to those who stand silent around her.

Attention paid to syntax, and in particular to the main verbs of each separate sentence, will show time and again how the sustaining motive or action of a speech flows underground at times, beneath the immediate and obvious sense of single words or subsidiary phrases. Displacement of words from their normal positions, contrasting parentheses, concluding phrases that are not essential for communication of purpose or pursuit of argument, sudden shifts of tense and abrupt changes in the person addressed, are some of the common signs of what actors, since Stanislavski's time, have learned to call 'subtext'. While a person in a play appears to be talking about one subject, his mind may all the time be fostering and developing other thoughts at a different, usually lower or less articulate, level of consciousness. These semiconscious, subconscious or, even, unconscious 'subtextual' reactions can be crucial for the development of the drama and the lifelikeness of speech and performance.

The most obvious example of subtext is when disguise requires the speaker to say one thing, whereas the real person beneath the disguise is thinking something quite different. So Iago sounds concerned and honest to Othello, Desdemona or Roderigo, but later he will acknowledge that under the text another thought, 'like a poisonous mineral', had gnawed his inwards (II i 291). Iago knows well how contrary thoughts can grow beneath the words that are spoken:

> Dangerous conceits are in their natures poisons
> Which at the first are scarce found to distaste
> But with a little act upon the blood,
> Burn like the mines of sulphur.   . . .   (III iii 330–3)

When, earlier in the same scene in Act III (lines 91–2), Othello says

> Excellent wretch! Perdition catch my soul
> But I do love thee   . . .

his conscious thoughts may be wholly confident and his words warm with satisfaction; but at another level of consciousness 'wretch' may register conflict and 'Perdition' insecurity. Perhaps even Iago does not know at this time how strongly such reactions are burning at hidden depths and are pressing Othello's spoken thoughts towards 'when I love thee not' and a 'chaos' of obliterating horror:

> Excellent wretch! Perdition catch my soul
> But I do love thee and when I love thee not
> Chaos is come again.

Subtextual realities have surfaced into textual suppositions, even though confidence and enjoyment are still the dominant notes.

So an actor becomes aware of how new elements of speech grow out of the undermining, unspoken thoughts; and how speech itself can change consciousness. A reader, too, may catch these flickering and then developing traces within the text, and so reach further into the speaker's inner being, its half-formed thoughts and strange unwilled fantasies.

In Shakespeare's text, a subtextual reality is nearly always present, although more in later than in earlier plays. When spoken words are forthright and simple, the motivation to speak them may not be talked about and not fully explicit in words. The main verb of each sentence can express the energy of spoken thought, often with remarkable completeness and clarity, but the movement towards that energy may be at yet another, deeper, silent level of being. It is not expressed in words, but has been built up through the performance as a whole and is set in motion by a total reaction to the total situation, moment by moment. What is said is only part of the drama of persons in speech and action.

One of the most engaging pleasures that Shakespeare's texts offer to a reader or an actor is the search for sustaining subtextual motivations: inner purposes, drives, and conflicts. A reader can be drawn into the very being of the speakers.

For example, when Desdemona, at the beginning of Act III, scene iii, persists in trying to restore Cassio to Othello's favour, she may seem perverse and tiresome, obsessed by a single idea and her own will:

DES.   Be thou assur'd, good Cassio, I will do
　　　All my abilities in thy behalf.
EM.　 Good madam do. I warrant it grieves my husband
　　　As if the case were his.
DES.   O that's an honest fellow. Do not doubt Cassio
　　　But I will have my lord and you again
　　　As friendly as you were.
CAS.　　　　　　　　　　Bounteous madam,
　　　Whatever shall become of Michael Cassio,
　　　He's never any thing but your true servant.
DES.   I know't. I thank you. You do love my lord;
　　　You have known him long and be you well assur'd
　　　He shall in strangeness stand no farther off
　　　Than in a politic distance.
CAS.　　　　　　　　　　　Ay but lady,
　　　That policy may either last so long
　　　Or feed upon such nice and waterish diet
　　　Or breed itself so out of circumstances,
　　　That I being absent and my place supplied,
　　　My general will forget my love and service.
DES.   Do not doubt that. Before Emilia here
　　　I give thee warrant of thy place. Assure thee
　　　If I do vow a friendship, I'll perform it
　　　To the last article. My lord shall never rest.
　　　I'll watch him tame and talk him out of patience,
　　　His bed shall seem a school, his board a shrift.

I'll intermingle everything he does
With Cassio's suit. Therefore be merry Cassio,
For thy solicitor shall rather die
Than give thy cause away.   (III iii 1–28)

In asking the basic question, 'Why does Desdemona use these words, in
this manner?', we must remember that in the first scene of Act III Emilia
has said that Desdemona has spoken already about this business that
morning and Othello has said already that in good time Cassio would be
restored to favour. So Desdemona promises here to do what in fact she
has achieved already, except for hastening the reconciliation. Then a
reader must consider what has happened to Desdemona: she has
recently awoken from her delayed marriage night; the wedding had
taken place in Venice, but the 'fruits . . . ensue' at Cyprus (II iii 9).
Much of the energy of her speech can derive from an awakened desire to
encounter with Othello in any way possible, on what ever occasion.
Cassio is someone else who 'loves' her lord, so she must be busy in that
'friendship' too. She must be the complete married woman: Emilia's
interjection at the beginning of the scene shows one wife sharing the
business of another, with a slight edge of rivalry or sense of comparable
power; and, in the same way, Desdemona suddenly refers to Emilia
again before giving Cassio 'warrant' of his place.

   Once the reader remembers that Desdemona's mind is full of the night
she has just spent with Othello, and that he is not with her at this
moment, her words will reveal new impulses and show that consciously
or unconsciously, in her fantasy, Desdemona is enjoying love-play with
her husband, eager, quick, combative, strong, pressing for advantage
and assurance, warm, generous, self-forgetful, delighting in every
prospect of encounter and fulfilment. Many of her words are found in
Shakespeare's plays at other moments of sexual arousal:
'*assur'd* . . . will *do* . . . *abilities* . . . will *have* . . . as *friendly* as you
were . . . have *known* him long . . . well *assur'd* . . . in *strangeness stand
no further off* . . . thy *place* . . . *Assure* thee . . . a *friendship* . . . *perform
it* . . . the *last article* . . . shall never *rest* . . . *watch* him *tame* . . . *out of
patience* . . . His *bed*[1] shall seem a school [i.e. he will there submit to
instruction, be under my control] . . . *intermingle*[2] . . . be *merry*
. . . *solicitor*[3] . . . *die*.' That last word is, perhaps, a conscious climax
to the subtextual run of Desdemona's thoughts, for the verb *to die*
was used very consciously by poets and writers – and for all we know by
ordinary lovers – as a synonym for sexual fulfilment; Shakespeare used
it in this way in *All's Well That Ends Well*, *Antony and Cleopatra*, *As You
Like It*, *Much Ado About Nothing*, *Romeo and Juliet* and in many of the
sonnets. The subtext of this whole passage is alight with sexual fantasy
and a sense of physical encounter that is new for Desdemona; Cassio

fails to make her aware of his own sense of the seriousness of his predicament. The subtextual strata of this encounter are unusually persistent in the text; perhaps Shakespeare allowed them to surface strongly in words because a 'boy actor' could not provide a full and life-like physical expression of such reality.

When Othello enters, Desdemona soon returns to the same theme. Almost at once he gives in to her – 'The sooner sweet for you' (line 57) – but Desdemona is impatient for the moment of gift. She delights in recollections of earlier differences that were expressed in merely teasing talk (see lines 71–5), but then vows 'I could do much'. Almost certainly, her thoughts are still on the night she has just spent with Othello. Again he gives in at once – 'I will deny thee nothing' – and so Desdemona's immediate purpose is achieved totally. Yet still she goes on talking: thinking and speaking now of everyday and intimate duties until her imagination runs ahead to further differences between them and far greater giving and taking in pursuit of their love together. Othello gives in to her a third time and now, when he asks her to go, Desdemona is proud to be the loser:

> . . .   Be as your fancies teach you;
> Whate'er you be I am obedient.   (III iii 89–90)

Their talk about Cassio has been love-play; in her 'fancies', Desdemona has been reliving the night together and letting her thoughts move backwards and forewards in time. Subtextually she carries off victory, and in performance this shines through the words that render victory to him.

A reader must always be alert to what the text says about performance beyond the strict meaning of its words or the speaker's conscious and explicit intentions. The first step is to seek out the heart of each sentence – each complete verbal activity – and observe how other thoughts forerun, coexist or follow after that. Every complicated sentence has shifts in the speaker's level of consciousness, and these will become clear in speech if the actor recognises and respects the basic syntactical structure. Complicated sentences are common in the plays because Shakespeare knew that human understanding was complicated and wanted to represent its several levels of consciousness. A reader needs to become as aware as an actor of this technique, otherwise he will skim off only a surface meaning. In the same way both actor and reader must watch for puns, double meanings and strange allusions or references, especially those that seem unconscious in the speaker; these, too, betray the mind within: the thought that is not consciously or explicitly expressed in words and yet influences speech and, still more, performance.

☆

Besides indications of subtextual impulses and developments, the text may contain implicit stage-directions that carry the speaker into states of mind and states of being that must so transform the manner of his speech that its very matter, or purport, will be changed from what it seems on a first reading with no thought of performance. This is very clear in the scene where Othello asks Desdemona for his handkerchief:

> OTH. I have a salt and sorry rheum offends me;
> Lend me thy handkerchief.
> DES.   Here my lord.
> OTH. That which I gave you.
> DES. I have it not about me.
> OTH. Not?
> DES. No faith, my lord.
> OTH. That's a fault. That handkerchief
> Did an Egyptian to my mother give.
> She was a charmer and could almost read
> The thoughts of people. She told her, while she kept it
> 'Twould make her amiable and subdue my father
> Entirely to her love, but if she lost it
> Or made a gift of it, my father's eye
> Should hold her loathely and his spirits should hunt
> After new fancies. She, dying, gave it me
> And bid me when my fate would have me wive,
> To give it her. I did so. And take heed on't,
> Make it a darling like your precious eye.
> To lose't or give't away were such perdition
> As nothing else could match.
> DES.   Is't possible?
> OTH. 'Tis true. There's magic in the web of it.
> A sybil that had numb'red in the world
> The sun to course two hundred compasses,
> In her prophetic fury sew'd the work.
> The worms were hallowed that did breed the silk
> And it was dy'd in mummy which the skilful
> Conserv'd of maidens' hearts.   (III iv 49–75)

In the early scenes of the play, Othello has been shown as a soldier and lover in complete command of himself and others. He is, in reputation

> . . . the noble Moor whom our full Senate
> Call all in all sufficient . . .   (IV i 261–2)

He is so much a part of the Venetian world that when Cyprus breaks out into a mutiny, he condemns the rioters from the established position of Christian civilisation:

> Are we turn'd Turk, and to ourselves do that
> Which Heaven hath forbid the Ottomites?
> For Christian shame, put by this barbarous brawl. . . . (ii iii 162–4)

Although Iago calls him an 'erring barbarian' and Barbantio argues that his daughter's marriage is 'against all rules of nature' (i iii 101), Othello's composure has been absolute and a whole army is proud to serve under such a 'full soldier' (ii i 36). But now, in this tale of the handkerchief, Othello speaks – very carefully and still in complete command – as if he were indeed a 'barbarian' and not a Christian, as if motivated by an enchantment which is against the acknowledged 'rules of nature'.

The exchange has numerous pauses at first, the last after 'That's a fault', because the verse-line is incomplete. But the next sentence runs over one line-ending and on to the end of the next verse-line. With this stronger thought and feeling come two words, 'Egyptian' and 'charmer', which introduce pagan and dangerous ideas. What follows at once could be fanciful superstition, but 'perdition' is a dangerous word meaning 'utter ruin' and, in a theological sense, 'damnation'. (As we have seen, it is a word that surfaced strangely in Othello's most intense joy; and here it is associated with 'darling', 'precious' and 'match'.) Desdemona's 'Is't possible?' is an incredulous and perhaps frightened interjection to which Othello responds with a candid ''Tis true': a phrase which is probably still more frightening in its simplicity. Without pause, he continues to speak of 'magic' and of the 'web' of the handkerchief – this latter a word that Shakespeare associated with fate and dangerous snares. Again the words are shockingly simple; but then, as if caught up in a forgotten world, the syntax and rhythms lengthen and a decorous, cosmic imagery suffuses his talk of a woman inspired by Apollo who had lived for two hundred years, of silkworms that were purified or held in veneration, and of a dye made out of hearts cut from the bodies of virgin girls.

To say all this, after those few short pauses, means that Othello now operates according to thoughts and feelings – at once tender, grand and terrible – that he has not acknowledged more than fleetingly at any earlier moment in the play. Unlike the angry, passionate cry for violent vengeance that had been his reaction when Iago made him think that Desdemona was unchaste, this passage is calm, assured and beautiful, and it dwells in the thoughts and feelings of his earliest years. The implications of Othello's words make huge demands upon the actor for innocence, strength, gracefulness and terror. Every word is affected: the pitch of voice, tone and volume; the kind of breath that vocalises the words; the expression and focus of Othello's eyes and, even, the coldness of his blood. In reading the text, the extreme grace of the lines and their calm rhythms can wholly occupy the mind; but a reader, like an actor, must recognise how innovative, deep and intuitive is the sustaining reality of Othello's inner being.

As the scene proceeds Shakespeare gives unmistakable signs that so much has been at stake. An instinctive cry from Desdemona, 'Then would to God that I had never seen it', triggers off an emotional reaction of a simpler kind: 'Ha! Wherefore?' The bare words must strike like lightning, suddenly charged by that deep power which has built up during Othello's account of the handkerchief; only after a terrible silence is Desdemona able to ask 'Why do you speak so startingly and rash?'. Then she founders, trying to hold on to rational talk from an earlier intimacy. Gripped now by his more violent feelings, Othello cries out, repeatedly, 'The handkerchief!' until he leaves the stage with the almost inarticulate oath, 'Zounds!' (line 98).

In scenes of strong feeling, Shakespeare frequently opposes two different reactions, as if the great force needed another, from a different source and often in a contrary direction, to hold it back and give a sense of building pressure until the final climax. In the eighteenth century, actors in the British theatre were especially conscious of these 'transitions' as they called them, creating especially daring theatrical effects to establish them as 'points' of power in Shakespeare's plays. A well known example is Shylock's alternation between hatred for Antonio and grief for the loss of his daughter. Whereas in the scene we have just studied in *Othello* one reaction succeeds another in textual expression, in *The Merchant of Venice* the two passions exist side-by-side, from one short speech of Shylock's to another in his exchange with Tubal:

> SHY.   . . . and no satisfaction, no revenge; nor no ill luck stirring but what lights o' my shoulders; no sighs but o' my breathing; no tears but o' my shedding!
> TUB.   Yes, other men have ill luck too: Antonio as I heard in Genoa . . .
> SHY.   What, what, what? Ill luck, ill luck?
> TUB.   Hath an argosy cast away coming from Tripolis.
> SHY.   I thank God, I thank God. Is it true, is it true? (III i 81-9)

The passions alternate, until Shylock is tortured with memories of his earliest love for Leah and then, at the next moment, takes practical steps to 'have the heart' of Antonio.

In very rapid alternations, this effect could become comical, but Shakespeare usually sets a slower pace. When Othello has actually seen Cassio and Bianca with his handkerchief, his first words are 'How shall I murder him, Iago?' (IV i 166). This is developed, under Iago's prompting, to 'I would have him nine years a-killing'. There may or may not be a silence following, for, like the scene of Shylock's tortured passion, this is in prose and so lacks the frame of metrical regularity. But certainly Othello takes hold of Iago's scorn of 'the foolish woman your wife'. Stubbornly, even against the tide of his revenge, those words sound again in Othello's mind and tap a contrary emotion of pity and love: 'A fine woman, a fair woman, a sweet woman.' From now on he oscillates, despite Iago's attempts to draw him one way (IV i 176 ff.):

IAGO   Nay you must forget that.
OTH.   Ay let her rot and perish and be damn'd tonight, for she shall not live. No, my heart is turn'd to stone; I strike it and it hurts my hand. O the world hath not a sweeter creature. She might lie by an emperor's side and command him tasks.
IAGO.   Nay that's not your way.
OTH.   Hang her. I do but say what she is: so delicate with her needle, an admirable musician. O she will sing the savageness out of a bear.   . . .

For a time Iago's interruptions have little effect, and Othello merely agrees, mindlessly:

. . . Of so high and plenteous wit and invention.
IAGO.   She's the worse for all this.
OTH.   O a thousand, thousand times. And then of so gentle a condition.
IAGO   Ay, too gentle.
OTH.   Nay, that's certain. But yet the pity of it, Iago. O Iago, the pity of it, Iago.

With the simple word 'pity', Othello turns to Iago, as if needing to be understood. The reply he receives sets the contrary stream of feeling running, more strongly than ever; and this time Othello's imagination fastens on the destruction of Desdemona, not of Cassio:

IAGO   If you be so fond over her iniquity, give her patent to offend, for if it touch not you, it comes not near nobody.
OTH.   I will chop her into messes. Cuckold me.

Now that his mind is fixed on the future and his own shame, it no longer oscillates but sharpens into immediate action.

Such a scene must be imagined step by step, as the words indicate the inward working of contrary feelings. With the cries, the quick mental reactions, the reiterations and contradictions, Othello's great body must shudder almost to destruction. The actor must trust absolutely to the words of each moment and hope that, after the alternations in imagination and feeling, the end of the scene will have some stability:

OTH.   Get me some poison Iago, this night. I'll not expostulate with her, lest her body and beauty unprovide my mind again. This night, Iago.

IAGO Do it not with poison. Strangle her in her bed, even the bed she hath
contaminated.
OTH. Good, good. The justice of it pleases. Very good.

Othello is cruel, but this 'pleases' him because for the moment he is
secure and almost calm: he can avoid more words; his imagination
contains both love and hate, her beauty and his determination, her
body and his. The end of this violent episode is probably very quiet:

IAGO And for Cassio, let me be his undertaker. You shall hear more by
midnight.
OTH. Excellent good.   (*A trumpet*)
What trumpet is that same?

In the stillness, Othello hears the voice of Venice and responds as if
nothing is out of the ordinary. In performance, his question can shock
an audience by its easy command. For a while, after Lodovico's
entrance, the strength of Othello's feelings are hidden, but when they
break out again it is in cruel violence against his wife. He is blind to her
suffering and leaves the stage almost at once, crying now against the
whole world: 'Goats and monkeys'. After fierce transitions of feeling
and their continuance under a temporary appearance of control, those
two words break out in savage hatred and wounded, frustrated love. A
reader will recognise the teeming sexual revulsion which they express
most blatantly, but the violence of the 'transition' and the brevity and
rhythm of the speech should also suggest that this savage speech and
action are forcing back a contrary sense of beauty, sweetness and fond
love.

Beneath the words on the page the physical and mental reality of the
persons of the drama is suggested. Every speech in the plays has to be
searched for indications of that continuing inner life, in so far as it may
be created by actors on stage and communicated to their audience. Not
only must words be heard as speech, but speech must be received as part
of a total, developing imitation of life. This is true as much of the
elaborate rhetorical speeches as of the almost inarticulate cries or the
silences implied by text and metre. Almost always there are several
ways in which a speech may come to life; but, while any one
performance will make its own selections, the options become progressively narrowed towards the end of the play. At last the force, weight and
authority of the inevitable may be achieved.

☆

The concluding moments of *Othello* provide a remarkable innovation in
the words that Shakespeare has written for the protagonist. Previously

Othello has acknowledged 'O hardness to dissemble' (III iv 31), but now, with 'Soft you, a word or two before you go', he is able to act out a formal summing-up of his life. Many of Shakespeare's characters have to perform like actors, but few of them do so like this, without preparation or apology. For a moment the surprise works totally, and Othello hides his inner feelings. But then the performance falters. As he speaks of

> ...   one whose hand,
> Like the base Indian, threw a pearl away
> Richer than all his tribe.   ...   (v ii 349–51)

he breaks down and weeps. Most editors print a long and irregular verse-line at this point, but Othello's words may be understood best as two incomplete lines. After a moment Othello recovers and acknowledges his tears as a sign of strange healing powers:

> Richer than all his tribe.   (*He weeps*)
>   Of one whose subdu'd eyes,
> Albeit unused to the melting mood,
> Drops tears as fast as the Arabian trees
> Their medecinable gum.   ...

He still further impersonates himself and then springs the last surprise of all, the secret purpose of his whole speech, the action for which all this dignified performance was only a cover:

> ...   Set you down this
> And say besides that in Aleppo once
> Where a malignant and a turban'd Turk
> Beat a Venetian and traduc'd the state,
> I took by th' throat the circumcised dog
> And smote him thus.

He kills himself, and a silence follows before anyone dares to speak. How that death is achieved is the actor's or the reader's choice – or rather it is a final clarification of the imaginative life that has been given to the play.

But the stroke of death is not quite the end. Othello has two more lines to speak, and they are a second innovation in the words of his part in this final scene. He uses only the simplest means:

> I kiss'd thee ere I kill'd thee. No way but this,
> Killing myself, to die upon a kiss.   (v ii 361–2)

After all the extraordinary words that he has spoken – tremendous and sensuous imagery, violent oppositions between 'tempests' and 'calms' and 'heaven' and 'hell', strong, slow-moving rhythms in the longer speeches, compact energy of commands, singing lyricism, relaxed humour, lightning strikes and open anguish – after the most demanding collection of words ever handed to an actor, Othello's last moments are contained in short phrases and a few words that clash one against each other. The life of the part, the very blood of the man, streams through the narrow gate, between *kiss* and *kill*, and *I* and *thee*. Othello may utter the words calmly or with passion: with a physical struggle to reach Desdemona's lips, or with an embrace that gives renewed strength to his voice and body. Or he can be incisive and almost unfeeling as he accepts the fate that has already haunted his mind. However the tightly phrased couplet is spoken, the actor must vindicate the words that challenge belief: 'No way but this'; and audience and readers must respond to the inevitability and destruction as fully as they are able. At the end of this tragedy Shakespeare ensures that his protagonist is viewed through a narrow aperture and into the depths of his being.

When we study Shakespeare's text we must be prepared for great variety. There is no one Shakespearean style: each play has its own style; and within each play, the style changes from speaker to speaker and scene to scene. Words and structure are often complex, representing subtle thoughts, conflicting emotions or hidden purposes. Often, speech rises on lyric melody, or veers quickly with sudden force, or almost stands still with secret and humane humour. On occasion, it is dangerously simple. The way through this fabulous world of words is to follow the *action* of the play, to maintain an imaginary, lively and physical reality for each person of the drama and to watch for hidden reactions until motive is clarified and words and actions have assured power.

10 | *Shows for Audiences*

I have argued that readers should become like actors and study how Shakespeare's words come alive in the act of performance. I have written at length about text because everything derives from that source, and I have considered the response of individual actors because that is where all the action starts. But now I want to establish an opposite and complementary point of view. Plays are written to be enjoyed by audiences, and this means that more than an actor's knowledge is required to understand them: a reader must also respond like an audience.

A play by Shakespeare is a concert of individual performances, a meeting, a process, a dance, a contest, an event, a microcosm. It has a structure, a shape, a body of its own that must be felt, a span of life that must be experienced in actual sequence and true proportion. A reader must be able to take it all in, as if confronted with a recognisable but unknown and strangely exciting world, and must understand when an onlooker is drawn into the drama, sharing the thoughts and experiences of each performer in turn, or when only one small detail catches attention, or when the whole wide stage is viewed as if from a distance or from a position of superior awareness. There will be moments when an audience identifies with only one person on stage and others when it is shut off from a secret happening or inhuman process. The illusion of another reality can be disturbed by undisguised artificiality or by the intrusion of a stronger actuality. Repetitions of words or actions, direct address to the audience or contrasting statements about a single event, are among the dramatic devices which invite ironic understanding or comic enjoyment. Early responses are displaced or revalued before the end of the play, and a sense of completion or final unmasking is an important element in the experience of an audience.

Frequent visits to many theatres provide the best way of learning how to appreciate the audience's point of view. But this does not mean that every student should fly off to see each new Shakespeare production that is known to draw the public, pleasurable though that might be.

Obviously such productions are especially enjoyable and instructive, but any theatre experience can increase a reader's understanding. Sensibility is strengthened through use and so, as our dramatic imaginations are exercised by going to all kinds of theatre, we will grow more able as we read to give substance to the drama that is hidden, waiting to be discovered, within the printed words of Shakespeare's texts.

Although no contact with the plays can equal that which is found in the theatres, I am not arguing that playgoing should supersede all reading of the texts. A reader has his own, very considerable, advantages. If we experienced Shakespeare's plays only in performance, our own explorations could be in danger of inhibition. A lack of contact with performance is no barrier to enjoyment and its possession no guarantee of full appreciation. We should see, hear *and* read the plays.

In the theatre we are not always free to encounter Shakespeare's created world. As we sit in the dark, ravishing scenic effects, realistic and busy elaboration of stage business, stunning rituals or carefully controlled and highly developed performances may make such effect upon our minds that the lively interplay of performance is lost to view and our own imaginations stifled. If a choice of two or three productions were offered and each one reputedly imaginative and talented, I would choose to go to the theatre where I could sit closest to the actors and so be able to enter, as well as view, the living world of the play. I would choose a new and adventurous performance rather than a production that had satisfied public opinion and had been running for months on end. This does not mean that the short-lived and small-scale, the fresh and the new, is always preferable. Shakespeare's imagination was vast as well as quick; those who stage the plays, as well as responding to immediate inspiration and the brightest, newest ideas, must also be ready to dig deep and take pains.

A reader or student who cannot visit theatres may have access to films of Shakespeare's plays. These are not simple equivalents to stage productions: they provide an alternative experience. What the director chooses to show through camera and soundtrack is a translation of the original into another medium. Cinemascope panoramas and close-up shots of human bodies can hide a great deal that is inherent in the texts. Variations of tempo and spatial relationships, strange perspectives, controlled colour and tone, and rapid cutting from shot to shot, are all foreign to the structure and substance of plays. What film offers is a strong filter through which to see the hidden life of Shakespeare's texts. Its distortion is both greater than that of any theatre production and also more noticeable; for that reason, it is sometimes very revealing. Besides, it offers a truer view than many other filters that are in common

use; because human persons can dominate a film directly and because the viewer is responsive to time in continuous performance, film is more in keeping with Shakespeare's imagination than most critical treatises which communicate only through the printed word.

One of the advantages of film is that two or three different versions can be viewed consecutively. So a student can compare one impersonation with another, the speaking of a single line in varied ways, different groupings of major figures or contrasted handling of crowds and stage-business. This will lead to independent enquiry about the truest implications of Shakespeare's text. Audiences who have shared a viewing of two films of *King Lear*, on two successive days, are very quick to talk among themselves afterwards, not so much about the films as about the play. Comparing different cinematic versions also increases the viewer's awareness of the film-maker's art and the varying distortions of his filter; this has the effect of encouraging a freer and more active engagement on the next occasion when the text of the play is read.

More recently television productions of Shakespeare's plays have become available on video-tapes. These have many of the qualities of film, but a smaller scale and cruder conditions of production mean that they are usually less fully achieved. Many of them are the result of only a few weeks' work with a group of actors who have not previously performed together. The best television Shakespeare has been made when a stage production has been redirected for the cameras, such as Trevor Nunn's *Antony and Cleopatra* and, especially, his *Macbeth*. In both cases the studio work has given a sense of fresh encounter to performances that have become deeply assimilated. The close-ups for soliloquies or duologues are particularly riveting and, in them, many of the limitations of television as a medium become advantages.

A further resource, when productions of plays or films are not accessible, is a workshop session in which a small number of skilled actors explore a play with which they are already familiar. Whole scenes can be read off-the-page, with movement and some action, and then played again at different tempos or with different actions, with alternative distances between members of a group, or with varied intentions or personifications. What is lost in force and precision in these rehearsal-like performances may be gained in fresh invention and the quick juxtaposition of opposed meanings and effects. Moreover a beginning of continuous action brings a sense of proportion, development and living engagement, which is easy to lose in a solitary reading of a text, however imaginative that may be.

Continuous performance is an absolutely irreplaceable dramatic quality which a student must not neglect. If productions, films, workshops or sound-recordings are all unavailable when investigating a particular play, then a reading of the complete text at one sitting should be attempted from time to time, preferably aloud. This will represent the shape and proportions of the drama and draw attention away from particular difficulties to the breadth and sweep of the whole. All the subtleties discovered in close study have to be related to such an experience, as careful details of orchestration in a symphony register at a remove from the reception of its main themes and structural development.

☆

Continuous performance establishes important facts about *Othello*. A reader will realise quickly enough that Iago dominates the play for the first two Acts; he starts the action and it is he who concludes three extended scenes in those acts with duologues and soliloquies that lead expectation forward and present him as self-conscious and dynamic. But the extent to which Othello carries the drama after that – by his strong emotional drives, desperate dissimulations, changing intentions and great range of physical actions – has to be experienced to be fully apparent. Laurence Olivier has said that the role of Othello is

> the biggest physical strain of all. . . . Admittedly you're not talking all the time, though you're sighing and groaning, and moving and making faces. In *Othello*, the passage from the handkerchief scene [III iii] through to flinging the money in Emilia's face is, pound by pound, the heaviest burden I know that has been laid upon me yet by a dramatist.[1]

Moreover, the dramatic focus becomes more and more intense in the last three Acts, with only a few brief episodes that have more than two, three or four persons on stage. It is this handling of the play's action which helped Shakespeare to introduce another unusual effect: repeatedly, in the last Acts, a silent figure holds attention, drawing eyes away from more active speakers and doers.

Sometimes the dialogue points explicity to the still centre: 'Behold her well; I pray you look upon her'; 'There lies your niece . . . I know this act shows horrible and grim . . . This sight would make him do a desperate turn'; 'Now, how dost thou look now? O ill-starred wench'; 'Look on the tragic loading of this bed' (v i 108; v ii 204–6, 210; v ii 275; v ii 366).

Elsewhere the very brevity of verbal interchanges concentrates the focus upon quiet, absorbed figures. Incomplete verse-lines mark the tense silences in:

OTH. Lend me thy handkerchief.
DES.   Here my lord.

OTH.	That which I gave you.
DES.	I have it not about me.
OTH.	Not?
DES.	No faith, my lord.
OTH.	That's a fault. That handkerchief . . . (III iv 50–5)

When Othello strikes Desdemona, incomplete verse-lines invite the
long pause that every actress in my experience has needed before
answering his 'Devil' with 'I have not deserv'd this' (IV i 236–7).
Another silence follows when Desdemona turns back and Othello waits
for Lodovico to speak. Then the dynamics of performance dictate yet
another, between Othello's 'You are welcome sir, to Cyprus' and the
cry of 'Goats and monkeys' in which his horror and anguish detonate
(IV i 260).

Only performance can reveal how frequently actors have to use the
many opportunities for intense silence. In Act IV, scene ii, Othello's
'Pray you chuck, come hither' (line 25) suggests that he attempts a
renewed intimacy so that he can search into Desdemona's eyes. But the
pain of his wounds is renewed with the closer contact and so he is soon
denouncing her repeatedly as a whore. Although he orders Desdemona
away, she stays close to him and his 'sense aches' at her very presence
(line 69). Only after this, as she continues to protest her innocence, may
he acknowledge a doubt:

OTH.	Are not you a strumpet?
DES.	No, as I am a Christian.
	If to preserve this vessel for my lord
	From any other foul unlawful touch
	Be not to be a strumpet, I am none.
OTH.	What, not a whore?
DES.	No, as I shall be sav'd.
OTH.	Is't possible?

That question stands alone, before the tide of the encounter presses
forward as before:

DES.	O heaven forgive us.
OTH.	I cry you mercy then.
	I took you for that cunning whore of Venice
	That married with Othello. . . . (IV ii 83–91)

Desdemona's use of 'us' after 'Is't possible?' may indicate that for one
precarious moment, after the incomplete verse-line, they have come
together in trust. Everything may hang in balance until she speaks
again. But then Othello, unable to bear contact with the body his

imagination has seen defiled, recoils in renewed revulsion. Without
pause, he calls, coarsely and impatiently, for Emilia, and then rushes
from the stage.

The dynamics of action in this play depends on such moments of
sudden, loaded stillness, and in performance each one of these feeds
upon the others. Later in the same scene, Iago encourages Desdemona
and Emilia to leave the stage. Now he is quite alone, as he has been often
enough in Acts I, II and III; but this time he does not speak in soliloquy.
His silence could be marked briefly before Roderigo enters. If so, his
parting words to Desdemona – 'All things shall be well' (IV ii 172) –
could give meaning to further unspoken thoughts: does he consider
what might be 'well' for himself? To be alone, perhaps? To be together
in trust had been good, momentarily, for Othello and Desdemona, and
this second silence could mark decisively the contrasting isolation of
Iago.

Many silences are unavoidable towards the end of the play. Such are
the moments of stillness during the singing of the Willow Song of 'poor
Barbara' while Desdemona gets ready for bed and is so quiet that she
hears a knock on the door. Even the cloak-and-dagger scene at the
beginning of Act v has its moments of quiet tension that offset the alarms
and cries of pain and loss. The last scene halts again and again, and each
time large issues are in the balance. The stumbling reactions of
Gratiano and Montano are used to show the oppressiveness of what is
seen and heard, before the narrative plunges forward once more:

EM.   My mistress here lies murdered in her bed.
ALL   O heavens forfend.
EM.   And your reports have set the murder on.
OTH.   Nay, stare not masters: it is true indeed.
GRA.   'Tis a strange truth.
MON.   O monstrous act.
EM.   Villainy, villainy, villainy.
        I think upon't. I think. I smell't. O villainy.   ...   (v ii 188–94)

A moment later Othello takes all attention with an inarticulate cry and
an impulsive, helpless action which, like a silence, leaves the audience
to sense the nature of his deep involvement:

OTH.   O. O. O.   (*Falls on the bed*)
EM.   Nay, lay thee down and roar
        For thou hast kill'd the sweetest innocent
        That e'er did lift up eye.   (lines 201–3)

When he is left alone, guarded by Gratiano, he catches the look in
Desdemona's face and approaches her dead body. He feels its coldness

and, almost immediately, falls silent. Nothing else happens until he cries out to curse and call for punishment. Then, once more, he becomes inarticulate; and then silent

> O Desdemona. Dead Desdemona, dead. O. O.   (line 284)

Nothing more happens until Lodovico enters; and his first words are 'Where is this rash and most unfortunate man?', so utterly still and quiet has Othello become.

The next silence is Iago's, who refuses, explicitly, to use words:

> Demand me nothing. What you know, you know.
> From this time forth I never will speak word.   (lines 306–7)

On at least two more occasions, before the end of the play, the audience on stage and in the auditorium will search Iago's face for some reaction: once when Cassio gives him the blame for Roderigo's part in the catastrophe; and once – or twice – when Lodovico's concluding speech calls for Iago to 'Look on the tragic loading of this bed' and then orders the new Governor to enforce his 'torture'. Some Iagos laugh and others maintain an inhuman inscrutability.

Othello's last moments, too, depend on actions rather than words. Having tricked his stage-audience into listening to a valedictory speech, he kills himself suddenly. There is a pause while the shock registers, and then Othello reaches towards Desdemona so that he may 'die upon a kiss'. That slow action, after the final words, locks them together in a final silence. Shakespeare has directed, by Lodovico's speech, that no one disturb this last view of their destruction and aspiration:

> The object poisons sight;
> Let it be hid. . . .   (v ii 367–8)

The bodies are not moved to be carried off-stage; the bed-curtains are drawn and then the play concludes.

In continuous performance, these still, intense, intimate and seemingly inevitable moments grow in power. Their effect is often accentuated by contrast with new actions introduced by other characters or by new speech-rhythms which break the lock, shatter the stillness, enforce, for a brief interval, a wider focus. But soon action and words seize up again: the protagonists are held or bound together because of what they are. The drama presses in upon an audience, offering little relief. There is no room for manoeuvre, almost every step seeming inevitable: what Emilia reveals is known already; when Desdemona recovers, she dies almost at once; her brave lie is accepted, but then denied; Othello's inability to escape –

> Man but a rush against Othello's breast
> And he retires . . .   (v ii 273–4)

– is because he has nowhere to go. Under such overwhelming and intense pressures individual affirmations are more striking and suggest deep resources: Desdemona's commendation to her 'kind lord' (v ii 128), Emilia's 'speaking as I think' (v ii 254), Iago's defiant isolation, and Othello's acceptance of his own tears, his self-identification with 'a malignant and a turban'd Turk', and his resolve that

> . . .   No way but this:
> Killing my self, to die upon a kiss.   (v ii 361–2)

These positives strike against the gathering silence, the freest and strongest movements of spirits that are confined by their own actions, passions and social relations. They reverberate in a heavy stillness from which no one, including the audience, can escape.

The quietness is all the more strange for the violence which has so often shaken the play. First is the destructive energy of Iago's mind, and then the passion of Brabantio for the loss of his daughter, followed by the brawl at night. The first counterstatement to this turbulence comes as Othello takes calm command, and he is again in control of the emergency meeting of the Senate. But then Iago takes the stage and the audience knows that:

> . . .   Hell and night
> Must bring this monstrous birth to the world's light.   (i iii 397–8)

The storm at sea, the 'high-wrought flood', follows pat on this cue, expressing a wider disorientation:

> What ribs of oak, when mountains melt on them,
> Can hold the mortise? . . .   (ii i 8–9)

Again there is a contrast, this time in news of the 'divine Desdemona' (ii i 73) and a calm at sea. On his arrival at Cyprus, Othello makes the comparison explicit in greeting his 'soul's joy':

> If after every tempest come such calms,
> May the winds blow till they have waken'd death,
> And let the labouring bark climb hills of seas
> Olympus-high and duck again as low
> As hell's from heaven. . . .   (ii i 183–7)

The end of the play is predicated in his next words:

> If it were now to die,
> 'Twere now to be most happy; for I fear
> My soul hath her content so absolute
> That not another comfort like to this
> Succeeds in unknown fate.   (187–91)

A secret happiness is now the centre of his being, and it is established as the central mystery of the whole play. Almost at once violence returns in the bonfires of celebration, Cassio's drunkenness, Roderigo's desperate efforts and, then, the 'wild' mutiny and 'dreadful bell' of the night alarm. Othello comes from his wedding bed and stills the uproar, but this time his mastery is not completely secure:

> My blood begins my safer guides to rule;
> And passion, having my best judgment collied,
> Assays to lead the way. . . .   (II iii 197–9)

When Desdemona follows him onto the stage, he tells her:

> All's well now, sweeting;
> Come away to bed. . . .   (II iii 244–5)

But his content will not be 'absolute' again – until, perhaps, at the very end of the play. He can 'deny' Desdemona nothing (III iii 77 and 84), and on this Iago builds his destructive action. Othello is made to suspect that he must lose Desdemona because he is 'black' (III iii 267) and uncivilised, and because he is older than she is; but his insecurity is deeper than such rationalising. His vision of Desdemona is heavenly and his desire infinite and free; and yet he is 'confined' (see I ii 27), a slave to limits and uncertainties. From now on he will 'shake' with terrible fancies, speak 'startingly and rash' and become insensible as he falls in a fit. He weeps and swears; cries 'Blood, blood, blood' and damns Desdemona – 'lewd minx' – repeatedly. But against this monstrous violence of body and spirit, Othello still holds on to love of Desdemona, recognising its power even as he prepares to kill her, and dying as he kisses her. Wonder, gentleness and trust ride out the labouring seas of distrust, passion and fear: his love has more than 'Promethean heat' and is not extinguished.

At the still centre is Desdemona. She has comparatively little to say, but everyone, including the audience, recognises her power. In the first three Acts, she makes only short appearances, depending on other people's business. The one exception to this is while she waits for

Othello to arrive at Cyprus and then, as she tells us:

> I am not merry; but I do beguile
> The thing I am by seeming otherwise. . . .   (II i 122–3)

Only when she prepares to go to bed as Othello has directed, and when he is waiting for the opportunity to murder her, can the audience know or share her intimate thoughts for more than a brief moment; and then it is Emilia who says most, while her mistress thinks about her whole life and that of all men and all women. Even here Desdemona keeps her secrets. Her husband's checks and frowns 'have grace and favour in them' (IV iii 19–20), mad Barbara and her song will not go from her mind, and her eyes itch which makes her think of weeping: these reactions are the surest guides to what she is. Her very simple words at the close of the scene are a kind of riddle:

> Good night, good night. God me such uses send,
> Not to pick bad from bad, but by bad mend.

Her forthright will has been evident before this – notably in her persistent championing of Cassio and her composure before the Senate and her father – but what she calls her 'soul', which she 'did . . . consecrate' to Othello, is known more by its effects than by its nature. Words that others use to describe it dazzle ordinary understanding: divine, heavenly, perfect, bounteous. Othello says, simply, 'the world hath not a sweeter creature' (IV i 180). She is like a light and other people like moths: Othello dies after loving her, and so do Brabantio, Roderigo and Emilia. Her power to attract is recognised by Iago, and used by him so that Cassio is wounded and he himself bound for torture. Although Desdemona has comparatively few words to speak, her part is crucial to the action of the play and in performance attention fastens progressively upon her. She exists at its quietest centre and is so presented that her very presence seems to offer both conflict and peace.

11 | *Stage Action*

To discover what a play shows an audience as all its action unfolds, a student should put himself in the place of a theatre director and ask what work is needed to stage the action and how the scenes will work together, draw interest forward and lead to a satisfying conclusion.

Some notion of a director's task can be gained by making lists of properties and stage-directions, and by working out groupings and movements by means of chessmen or other manikins, as I have suggested before. (See page 55 above.) But a director, or a group of actors working together, has to take these issues much further and consider how one choice influences another and how the whole play fits together. A student will find it helpful to make decisions: what kind of bed should Desdemona and Othello have? Where should it be placed on stage, and how does it get placed there? What happens to it when Desdemona struggles for life? How far does Othello have to reach to kiss her upon his death? Does he give way to tears while he is still standing up? What instrument does he use to kill himself, and where has it been concealed? Is he dressed ready for bed or as he appeared in the streets of the previous scene? Does he bring a candle on stage or is it standing at the side of the bed? Each one of these decisions is liable to affect the others, and a student or theatre director who answers them responsibly will gain a grasp of the entire play.

Perhaps the best way to start is to take one scene and try to decide every practical detail for that. Seek out illustrations, drawings or actual costumes for everyone on stage. Photographs of modern dress are easier to find than illustrations of period clothes, and may be a greater spur to imagination; besides, in his own day Shakespeare's plays all had modern dress. Choose one out of three, four or five possibilities and ask how the choice affects other aspects of the play in action, in terms of use, style, colour-contrast, form and material. Get pictures of each stage-property that will be used; determine its size, weight, material, shape. Work out groupings and movement for every character at every moment in the scene.

Students may find it helpful to devise actions and choose costumes for a stage-setting that has been seen in a current production; but it is advisable to choose one that was used for another play and not for the one that is being studied. Alternatively, an entirely new stage-set can be designed for a particular theatre that the student knows well. Of course, the theatres we visit today use modern staging methods, very unlike those imagined by Shakespeare; and so it is particularly interesting to work out the dynamics of a play's action on a board representing the shape and proportions of the platform stage of the Globe or the open stage of the Blackfriars Theatre. The various entry doors can be marked and an upper level provided. This reconstruction of physical stage-conditions need not involve complete historicity of costumes, properties or behaviour; in these aspects, an immediate, lively response should be sought at the start of any physical exploration of a play.

All investigations should be as practical as possible. Not only should pictures of costumes, properties and stage-setting be found and brought together, but models can be constructed, snippets of actual materials collected, and chessmen moved to appropriate positions. When a specific action or gesture is required, a student can experiment by enacting them himself and speaking the accompanying lines at the same time. More elaborate stage-business or rituals – such as fights, meals or funerals – will have to be left to imaginary realisation, but some part of them can also be enacted, possibly in slow motion. As in the exploration of speech, all such work should stop far short of performance: a student needs a cool mind to assess what is happening and is not equipped to cross the frontier between going through the motions of a play and actually performing it. Such a limitation still leaves a good deal to be accomplished, and all this work can both add to an understanding of the dramatic implications of a text and feed a student's imagination. In this way a 'world' is possessed and the words of the dialogue live in the three-dimensional, physical inter-relationships of the persons of the drama.

More specialist functions may be especially stimulating to some readers. A musician should try to choose or compose music, and then record and play it to accompany a reading of the text. A fencer can learn about renaissance sword-play and devise an actual combat. Someone with appropriate equipment and expertise in sound-effects could work on the storm scene in *Lear* or *The Tempest*, using first realistic sound and then invented, expressive equivalents. None of this will provide 'correct' solutions, but an extension of reading and study should be achieved which encourages a fuller realisation of the physical elements of the drama.

Once several scenes have been explored in this practical dimension, a student is ready to tackle a whole play and, with it, many new problems. Casting is perhaps the first that should be attempted. To be useful this, too, must be practical and decisive. A play can be cast from actors known to a student; film and television have made most of us familiar with many excellent performers and we can choose from these. A name – and a few press-photographs – should be put against each part in the cast list; and it is useful to justify every choice at different moments in the play against informed criticism. Another way of casting is to use, not actors but, individuals who are known in public or daily life and to imagine them speaking particular lines. The choice of one role to play oneself can lead to the actual speaking of the lines of the part to see where the greatest difficulties arise. Obviously, a particular kind of imagination is needed for all this work, but many people possess it; and we have some practice for it in day-dreaming about experiences other than our own.

Another exploratory exercise is to ask how two or three hundred lines could be cut from the text of the play, and to work out the consequences of two or three different solutions. Problems of exposition, narrative and dramatic development will be confronted by this means and precise issues raised. Similar issues are raised by asking where it would be possible to introduce one or two intervals in a performance and, again, comparing the effect of different decisions. The fact that the Globe Theatre had no intervals only makes this process more instructive, because there is no one satisfactory answer to the problem. However, the plays were printed with act and scene divisions and these do provide a start for any study of the play's structure. It can be helpful to write down an abstract of what happens in each scene and act, and a list of the aims of a production in each one of these sections. The shorter such descriptions are, the more challenging this kind of study.

The further a reader can travel into practical and detailed work, the more difficult the decisions will become and the more engrossing. In a very few days a practical student will have accumulated a great mass of material and many notes of decisions, so that some reappraisal and sorting out will have to be done. It is probably time to stop collecting and let the play live more freely in one's imagination, returning to particular problems later.

Some books about producing Shakespeare can be read with profit at this stage – but not earlier, because they may inhibit independent thought. I recommend studies that are particular rather than general, and 'Suggestions for Further Reading' provide references to a number of these. Among general books, Peter Brook's *The Empty Stage* (1968, and many times reprinted) raises the most basic questions about performance styles. In *Free Shakespeare* (1974) I have tried to describe production methods that respond to the qualities of Shakespeare's texts and also the conditions of performance in his own day.

☆

Much Ado About Nothing was one of the first new plays at the Globe Theatre after its opening in 1599. It affords a fair example for showing how lively entertainment is implicit in Shakespeare's text.

In the first ten minutes the stage fills and clears several times, the dialogue shifts from prose to verse and back again, the plot is set in action, and surprises start to register. Two young women enter first and they are met at once, probably from the opposite door, by Leonato, the elderly Governor of Messina. A young military Messenger is in attendance who has brought a message announcing the return of the Prince, Don Pedro, after a successful expedition against his bastard brother, Don John; an insurrection has been put down and excitement is in the air. The first words are Leonato's, to his young daughter, Hero, and his niece, Beatrice. Within seconds the talk is about two young men, Claudio and Benedick, who will be coming with Don Pedro. Now Beatrice joins in and has far more to say than the man who has brought the news. She awakens quick laughter and everything becomes a little 'mad'. Then, before anyone realises it, Don Pedro is on stage. With him are the young officers and others, among them Don John who has been reconciled to his brother. The stage is full now, and noisy with the sounds and sights of soldiers returned from war and looking for relaxation. The long dresses of the young women no longer dominate the scene, but the clothes and weapons of the travel-stained soldiers. Everyone moves to welcome the royal guest, the ladies and their attendants curtseying low. After a moment's pause, Don Pedro speaks and the ice is broken. He turns to be introduced to Hero and again laughter is in the air. While he talks with Leonato, unheard by the others or the audience, Beatrice singles out Benedick and they talk together like practised duellists looking for advantage.

The stage is crowded and busy for only a few minutes. Then Leonato and Don Pedro go off together followed by everyone except Claudio, who holds Benedick back from following the prince. Having made sure they are alone, Claudio talks of Hero in such a solemn, urgent way that Benedick laughs, interrogates his young friend and ridicules his romantic fervour. Unexpectedly, Don Pedro returns, looking for Claudio, and Benedick gets his commander to order him to tell the secret. It is soon told and Benedick is sent off now, all in good spirits as he plays the part of a dutiful subordinate. Alone with the Prince, Claudio declares his love for Hero, whom he has seen only briefly on his way to war, and lively prose gives way to measured verse. The Prince promises to speak for Claudio and ask for Hero's hand in marriage, and they go off together. Don Pedro proposes to speak when everyone is in disguise at the masked revel or ball that is due that night; and he will pretend to be Claudio. So with only two people on stage in private and urgent conference at the end of the first scene, the first flurry of jests and play-acting yields to far more serious talk of impersonation and intentional confusions.

The play reverts to prose in the second scene and Leonato is seen meeting another old man, his brother Antonio, and enquiring busily of him about music for the dancing. In return he is told that Claudio and Don Pedro have been overheard talking together. This is a further complication, because the impression has been given that it is the Prince, and not Claudio, who loves Hero. Leonato half disbelieves all this, but becomes still more urgent and busy. Antonio is sent off on an errand, and Leonato follows a moment later, stopping only to order nameless attendants and relatives to do this and that as they rush back and forth in preparation for the celebrations. This busy and confusing scene takes only a minute or so to perform, but provides a total contrast for the next in which Don John enters resentful and brooding. He plans to do nothing and the action is at a stop while Conrade, one of his followers, tries to talk him into better spirits. Don John speaks only to confirm his hatred of everything, but he is alert to the silent entry of Borachio, another of his men. News is given of the royal entertainment and the impending marriage. Borachio has got it right and knows Claudio to be the suitor. Once more there is laughter, but this time it is sour and malicious. The three go off, intent on crossing the happiness of others. So closes Act I.

The play has started with a number of quick and varied encounters, each establishing divergent purposes and different assumptions. When the principals re-enter at the start of Act II, all are dressed in their finest clothes. Music plays for dancing and masks are put on – probably grotesque faces, in the fashion then current. Possibly torches are brought on stage as well, for it is night-time, and soon the stage is full with at least four pairs of dancers. There must be quiet attention before the dance begins and at this time the audience will see an almost complete line-up of the persons in the play. Then dance enlivens the stage, varied as some couples stop dancing briefly, for talk and laughter. As the masquerade continues out of sight, the stage is cleared, except for Don John, Borachio and (at some distance) Claudio, none of whom has joined in the entertainment. After some words spoken out of the young lover's hearing, Don John crosses to Claudio and, pretending that he thinks he is Benedick, tells him that Don Pedro has wooed Hero as his own bride. He leaves and, in verse once more, Claudio speaks the first soliloquy of the play, so that his sharp sense of betrayal and loss registers strongly and inescapably with the audience. At this point Benedick reappears in the cheerful belief that his friend has been spared the torments of being a lover. He finds Claudio in a quite different mood, uncommunicative and brusque. Benedick is soon left alone for *his* first soliloquy; he speaks of Claudio as 'a poor hurt fowl' and goes on to reveal that he, himself, has been hurt by the taunts which Beatrice had delivered to him when he was masked.

The corporate comedy has given way to two contrasted cries of surprise and new resolution. Then Don Pedro and, soon after, Leonato and Hero return, all elated with the dancing and excitement of impending marriage. Claudio has been brought back by Beatrice, and a moment later Leonato betrothes Hero to her true suitor. At this point, with everyone gathered round, Claudio has nothing to say. Only when Beatrice prompts him does he pledge his love. Then another silence falls, and Beatrice prompts Hero. She then relents and sets everyone laughing as the two lovers kiss in happy, private silence. No moment in the play so far has been so intimate and so absolutely lifelike. On the top of renewed laughter, Don Pedro speaks to Beatrice – 'In faith, lady, you have a merry heart' – and the next series of incidents is set in motion.

The first section of the play is complete now (at the close of Act II, Scene i). Across the arena of the stage there have been continual movement and changes of mood, but, from time to time, individual intentions have been stated unequivocally. Now the tempo changes and some scenes are sustained for longer confrontations. But still there is 'much ado', until the very last minutes of the comedy when Benedick and Beatrice are also betrothed and, like Claudio and Hero before them, are silenced with a kiss.

Before the comedy is rounded off so happily, the action has to take many different turns. Each scene reflects on the others with sharp efficiency, and soliloquies or duologues provide contrasting moments of strong and, sometimes, destructive feeling, and so arouse deeper, dangerous excitements. Benedick conceals himself as Claudio, Pedro and Leonato talk about him and say how desperately Beatrice is in love with him. He is fully visible to the audience, however, and speaks aside in their hearing as he watches this 'play' put on for his benefit – for the talk is all a trick to make Benedick fall in love. The others leave hurriedly once their job is done, so that they shall not spoil the effect by laughing outright. Then Beatrice is caught by Hero and her gentlewoman, Ursula, in much the same way, except that she keeps everything bottled-up until left alone. Both find themselves on the threshold of a kind of 'folly' (II iii 214), with a new 'appetite' (II iii 217) or 'fire' (III i 107) in their minds.

The other plots develop dangerously, too. Don John makes Claudio believe that Hero has already had an affair with Borachio, and so the formalities of an elaborate wedding-scene are disrupted by the bridegroom's bitter denunciation of the bride. By this time a very funny scene has shown the local watchman overhearing the drunken Borachio tell about the trick played on Claudio. Before the wedding Don John's two henchmen have been arrested and their trial follows conducted by

Dogberry, the absurdly self-confident Constable. But meanwhile, the action has plunged further into high drama, for in front of the church altar, after everyone else has left, Benedick finds Beatrice alone and weeping. She is outraged by what the men have done, and in the play's most passionate scene asks Benedick to kill Claudio for slandering her cousin. Benedick had stayed behind out of concern for Beatrice's tears, and as he faces her passionate anger he also – almost in spite of himself – declares his love for her.

A director who tries to describe all the action of *Much Ado*, as it would be seen and heard in performance on a platform stage will need more words than are spoken in the play. New tricks follow others, catching attention in contrary directions. As in Shakespeare's other comedies, an abundant invention gives to the action an infectious vitality. This is all the more pervasive in that each new turn is handled with deft economy.

At the end, just before the last tangles of the plot are unravelled, a short scene (v iii) creates a wholly new kind of dramatic illusion. By now Claudio knows that he has accused Hero falsely, but he also believes she is dead from the shock and shame of what has happened. With Don Pedro he enters Leonato's family monument, late at night and accompanied by servants carrying tapers. Every one is silent as he reads an epitaph in verse and hangs the scroll on the tomb. Then solemn music follows and a small choir sings a hymn to the 'goddess of the night'. At no time has the stage been so still and death-like; singers, musicians, Claudio, the Prince and attendants, all stand dressed in black, their heads bowed. If the play was performed at Shakespeare's Globe Theatre in winter, afternoon light would be failing by this time, and when Don Pedro broke the silence to ask for lights to be extinguished, the play's imagined dawn might in fact be the half-light of a winter's evening touched by a setting sun. Nothing breaks the new slow tempo, until the stage is emptied and the 'tomb' is either hidden by curtains at the rear of the stage or moved off by the stage-keepers. Then the action springs to life again as the other characters enter to restore Hero to Claudio and to see Benedick married to Beatrice – although even Benedick cannot be quite sure that this will happen and, certainly, he is not ready to announce it.

The last scene, finishing in a dance for everyone, is short, but before its end the happy progress is halted three times. First, when all the ladies enter in a row, masked as they were for the ball at the beginning of Act II, and Claudio has to take one of them for his wife. As he hesitates his insecurity must return; and it is some time before he knows that Hero has been restored to him. Then, when Beatrice and Benedick are about to acknowledge that they love each other, at the last moment both deny it. The action stands still again until both are convicted of love by the testimony of poems each has written to the other. Finally, as music starts for the concluding dance, it is suddenly stopped by the entrance of a military messenger. All eyes turn to the breathless figure who has just dismounted from his horse and stands in stark contrast to the wedding-guests in all their finery. This messenger is the first to speak and reports that Don John has been captured. Everyone laughs with pleasure, but when music starts again and the comedy concludes with one more dance, an additional brightness and energy may express how precarious and how forgetful of everything else is the happiness that is then celebrated.

Much Ado is like other comedies by Shakespeare in the way that its dramatic focus changes all the time. At certain moments, the audience identifies intensely with the principal persons, however much they have laughed at their words and actions. At other times – as in the dances, the entry to the wedding-service and the ritual mourning at the tomb – individuality is almost lost in a general shift of mood and formal unified movements. These are transformation scenes, in which intentions and feelings are concealed and may, perhaps, change. They have a pervasive and cumulative effect on the audience, so that when Claudio goes to claim his second bride, 'were she an Ethiope' (v iv 38), a formal gesture can act as reminder that he is no longer the Claudio who is half-afraid 'to drive liking to the name of love' (I i 262): the dark scene at the family monument has changed all that, and the audience will see how only Hero brings full life to him now. Benedick and Beatrice shy away from marriage rites, but Beatrice is silent and complaisant when he calls out 'Strike up, pipers', the last words of the play that dismiss all thoughts of conflict for that last show of happiness. The audience will enjoy the dance but may also watch its leaders with a special understanding: mad, tumultuous, dangerous and individual feelings lie underneath the show of harmony.

No verbal statement can provide a satisfactory clue to a play by Shakespeare. It is tempting to think that *Much Ado* shows how men and women 'suffer love' against their wills (v ii 56–8) or how men, as these women say, are 'turned into tongue and trim ones too' (IV i 316–17) and make much ado when they should be able to 'see a church by daylight' (II i 70). But as verbal clues are part of full performances, so each action lives and registers its meaning in relation to that of the whole play. The proper function of every moment of the drama belongs to its appropriate context; and its effectiveness and meaning depend upon placing and proportion. The last kiss in *Much Ado* – or its last dance or last image of blackness and death – is one of a sequence, and out of its proper position its very nature would change, and the nature of the audience's reception. Moreover, every detail serves the sure movement of the whole comedy towards a resolution that was predicated, lightly and thoughtlessly, from the very first time anyone entered on stage.

In the same way, *Hamlet* cannot be summed up by any of Shakespeare's words or by any single moment. The killing of the King is part of a sequence of changes in the Prince and in his understanding of himself. Indeed the play is, in part, a series of summings-up, each one cancelled in due turn and with varying force:

> . . . I have that within which passes show;
>
> Angels and ministers of grace defend us –
>
> The time is out of joint. O cursed spite
> That ever I was born to set it right.
>
> . . .   'Tis a consummation
> Devoutly to be wish'd: to die, to sleep;
>
> . . .   Now could I drink hot blood,
> I'll lug the guts into the neighbour room.
>
> . . . Man and wife is one flesh;   . . .
>
> . . .   I do not know
> Why yet I live to say 'This thing's to do';
>
> I lov'd Ophelia;   . . .
>
> . . .   Is't not perfect conscience
> To quit him with this arm?   . . .
>
> Hamlet is of the faction that is wrong'd;
> His madness is poor Hamlet's enemy.
>
> But let it be.   . . .   1

Any one of these moments can seem to hold the secret of the play as it is performed; but verbal statement cannot define the tragedy. Each moment, in its full realisation, is always a part of something other than itself: the whole play. *Hamlet*, like any other organism, is always changing, and the secret of its life will always remain a mystery. Our closest definitions will be in terms of its stage-life – the whole of it as we can appreciate it with our best enquiry and imagination.

Friedrich Nietzsche was particularly concerned in his philosophical writings with origins and ultimate meanings. He believed that any sensitive spectator of ancient tragedy would experience 'the need to look and at the same time go beyond that look'. To him, writing in 1872, tragedy seemed to 'hide as much as it revealed', and he longed to tear away the surface and discover the reality, some other sense of being that was like music and inspired hope:

Our study of the genesis of Greek tragedy has shown us clearly how that tragic art arose out of music, and we believe that our interpretation has for the first time done justice to the original and astounding meaning of the chorus. Yet we must admit that the significance of the tragic myth was never clearly conceptualised by the Greek poets, let alone philosophers. Their heroes seem to us always more superficial in their speeches than in their actions: the myth, we might say, never finds an adequate correlative in the spoken word. The structure of the scenes and the concrete images convey a deeper wisdom than the poet was able to put into words and concepts. The same may be claimed for Shakespeare, whose Hamlet speaks more superficially than he acts, so that [an] interpretation of *Hamlet* . . . [has] to be based on a deeper investigation of the whole texture of the play.[2]

Neither character-analysis nor statement of theme expresses the dramatic experience adequately. Structure, texture, music, madness, beauty, sublimity are some of the words that Nietzsche used to capture its essence, and for Shakespeare's plays similar ones will be needed. The continuous show must be part of any understanding: sequence, timing, proportion, repetition, rhythm, sights, shows and continuous and varied action, are quite as significant as anything that may be said at any particular moment.

But Nietzsche's terms are insufficient for Shakespeare's plays. I suspect that we will each find in our own lives and imaginations the most useful ways of talking about the experience that they provide. The plays do not lead me to think of music, inhuman forces, pure events or super-heroes: they heighten my awareness of living, rather than transcend it.

Shakespeare was not only imaginative himself, but the cause of imagination in others. His plays should be performed in a space which the audience can both observe and share. Their silences must be protected and the text allowed to set the actors in motion with every freedom that talent can use. Each performance is a shared exploration and re-creation: our own imaginations, as well as Shakespeare's and the actors', give life to the plays; our own experiences, and the ideas by which we try to understand them, help to define what we see in the mirror held up to nature. The fantasy of the plays is also real, a bettering of nature,[3] that shows us ourselves in exterior and interior life.

12 | *Context*

When we considered individual words as part of performance, we took into account the place that Shakespeare occupies in the history of the English language so that we could recognise meanings that are now lost. In the same way, Elizabethan stage-practice and the shape of early theatres informed our discussion of the plays in action before an audience. This historical perspective is appropriate for every aspect of these studies. No matter how easily a text leaps to life in our imaginations, a knowledge of its original context in Elizabethan and Jacobean England can amplify that experience. It may lead us to discover further forces and excitements within the action, refine our understanding of personal and intellectual issues, and deepen our appreciation of dramatic structure and resolution. While the recovery of lost meanings and implications is no substitute for an imaginative and active exploration of a play, and while we can never react like an Elizabethan audience, a study of the minds and lives of Shakespeare's contemporaries can alert us to factors that have been obscured or modified with the passage of time and so heighten our sense of discovery.

Plenty of books are ready to help. Twentieth-century critics have devoted many years to historical reconstruction and have published the more tangible and verifiable results of their researches. Politics, economics, morality, philosophy, religion, iconography, historiography, psychology, medicine, education, rhetoric, esthetics are some of the subjects that have been explored in their Renaissance manifestations in order to reveal original meanings and to seek out Shakespeare's intentions. Books that Shakespeare himself read, especially the 'sources' of each play, have been carefully sifted to discover what he copied and what he rejected. Records of his life and those of his family, friends and associates have been examined minutely to develop understanding of his concerns and achievements: and reflections of all this experience have been sought within the plays.

Evidence about Shakespeare's England and opinions about its

relevance to the plays are stacked in a bewildering mass in every modern library. A guide through the labyrinth is needed and numerous versions have been provided. Perhaps the most convenient are the select bibliographies printed in single-volume editions of each play. But a wider selection, including books on more general topics, will be found in *Select Bibliographical Guides: Shakespeare*, edited by Stanley Wells (1973) or in *A New Companion to Shakespeare Studies*, edited by Kenneth Muir and S. Schoenbaum (1971). The fullest of several bibliographies that are published yearly, after each new crop of Shakespearean scholarship, is in the American periodical, *Shakespeare Quarterly*. This gives brief descriptions of each item. A more evaluative, though more selective, guide is published in Cambridge in the annual *Shakespeare Survey*.

Few English-speaking people can have passed through school to the age of sixteen without becoming aware of the existence of all this scholarship, even though they may have read none of it. Students for whom English Literature is a subject until school-leaving at eighteen will know, at first hand, a few of the more popular literary and historical studies. The verbal definitions of character, meaning and intention that are found in these books describe Shakespeare's plays in his own time more confidently than they assess them in our own. By their means, readers absorb a great deal of information about the original context of the plays and may find that their own reactions to the texts are thereby clarified and rationalised. More works of historical criticism are added every year to our resources.

But, as an awareness of the plays in performance leads to a new kind of enquiry about Shakespeare's words and their theatrical effectiveness and consequences, so it raises new questions about the experience, ideas and sources that contributed to the composition of the texts. Once the plays are read and enjoyed in their full stage-life, a student will turn afresh to books of historical research with his own questions – precise enquiries which many of the learned writers may have never foreseen. Persons in action, which are the heart of the matter, have a relationship to their historical context which is not to be defined by reviving old arguments or marshalling verbal statements. The information presented in historical studies has to be related to a lively engagement in the life of the plays, an action which mirrors the very form and pressure of Shakespeare's own times.

It must be confessed that some of the most thorough and discriminating books that have been written about Shakespeare's plays are literary or philosophical, rather than theatrical or imaginative. An assumption that the meanings of words on a page are the limits of a student's curiosity is surprisingly common, and a thorough attention to it can frustrate attempts to enquire further. Perhaps an open and lively study of a text is best supplemented by neglecting interpretative historical studies in favour of some of those books that Shakespeare himself read while writing it or some other books which were most influential in his own day. There are good modern studies of the philosophical ideas that can be traced in *Hamlet* or *The Tempest*, but when we are stimulated by an experience of what happens in those plays, a reading of John Florio's translation of Montaigne's *Essays* (especially those sections which are echoed in the plays) will provide ideas and phrases that pass directly into our own engagement with the play's action.

Fortunately, Shakespeare's sources and the great books of the Renaissance are now readily available, and comparatively cheaply: we can enter the intellectual world which Shakespeare knew and explored in his plays. For *King Lear* we can read, as Shakespeare did, Sir Philip Sidney's *Arcadia*, Raphael Holinshed's *Chronicles* and the earlier, anonymous play of *King Leir*. To these we should add *The Book of Job* in the Bible, Erasmus's *The Praise of Folly* and, for a better understanding of Edmund's ambition and intelligence, Machiavelli's *The Prince* or, better still, his *Discourses*. These books will enlighten our understanding of many other plays as well, for they are seminal works: *The Book of Common Prayer* and the *Homilies* of the Established Church; the works of Bacon, Hooker, Calvin, Aquinas, Seneca, Plato; Sir Thomas Wilson's *Art of Rhetoric*, George Puttenham's *Art of English Poesie*; Foxe's *Book of Martyrs*, Sir Thomas More's *Utopia*, the collaborative *Mirror for Magistrates*, or Castiglione's *Courtier* in Sir Thomas Hoby's translation; the works of the poets Chaucer, Spenser, Ralegh and Donne; the plays of Marlowe, Lyly and Jonson; the various writings of Nashe, Greene, Dekker and Heywood.

In a single paragraph I have suggested a life-time's reading. Of course everyone must be selective and must rely sometimes on the reports of scholars who have explored Renaissance thought and art with careful attention over many years. I urge only that everyone caught up in the study of Shakespeare's plays should spend some time reading what he read, skipping where necessary and following more specific clues when these are available. When studying one of the tragedies or some of the later history plays, a start could be made with a few comparatively short and accessible works that are of utmost importance: Erasmus, *The Praise of Folly*, Montaigne's 'Of Canibals' and 'An Apology of Raymond Sebond' from the *Essays*, and the greater part of Book One of Machiavelli's *Discourses*. To these should be added the actual sources that Shakespeare used during composition.

Earlier English and Renaissance plays are a very special kind of source. Here Shakespeare could have learnt about dramatic form and convention; and here he developed his own sense of the possibilities of theatre. Some excellent books, together with a reading of the plays themselves, offer views of this wide territory; they are listed in 'Suggestions for Further Reading' at the conclusion of this book.

But the plays sprang from the experience of living as well as from thought and literary endeavour. Paintings, woodcuts, architecture (including the arrangement of living-space in houses and apartments), furniture, ornament, dress, music, sports, carnivals, legal procedures, financial arrangements, formalities and regulations of all kinds, the practice of medicine, education, apprenticeship, military training, agriculture, trade, worship, burial, the daily lives of the poor and homeless, and of the royal, rich, noble, learned, skilled, superstitious and ignorant: knowledge of all this, and much more, can inform our understanding of the life of the plays. Once again, the quest is, happily, endless, to the enrichment of our speculation and imagination. But time is short and opportunity limited.

The best way to begin may be to look at pictures, and at buildings where these are neither altered too much nor restored too inhumanly. Music of the period can be heard from recordings in both modern and reconstructed styles of performance. Social histories and reprints of documents about day-to-day life are further aids which can flesh out suggestions in the texts. Marriage, childbirth, parental authority and inheritance are frequently crucial to the action of the plays, and there are now several good and detailed studies of these matters. Useful accounts of many aspects of Elizabethan and Jacobean life are provided in an illustrated and well-documented work published (in two volumes) in commemoration of the three-hundredth anniversary of Shakespeare's death, and still in print: *Shakespeare's England: An Account of the Life and Manners of His Age*, edited by Sir Sidney Lee and C. T. Onions (1916). This valuable survey has been supplemented by accounts of court-life, foreigners in England, apprenticeship, law, prisons, dissent, science, folklore, publishing, music, language, and so on, in *Shakespeare in His Own Age* edited by Allardyce Nicoll; first published as volume 17 of *Shakespeare Survey* in 1964, it is now available in paperback.

Again, the student has a vast field for exploration and will need to use indexes and encyclopaedias to narrow the search. The study of plays in performance often raises very precise questions that lead a student beyond general and descriptive accounts. Notes in modern editions of the texts are of little use. Most editors are not aware of the problems of performance and do not attempt to give information about what might happen, actually, when Laertes and Hamlet fight with sword and rapier, or what the texts suggest might happen to Lear's body as he dies; how Friar Francis might begin to conduct the marriage ceremony in *Much Ado*, or what exactly was provided for Juliet's bedroom, or how the torches were managed at a dance. Students will have to search for themselves in reprints of early books or documents, or in reproductions of paintings and book illustrations. All this takes a good deal of time, even with practice in following the clues of footnotes and bibliographies, but the effort can be enjoyable when it leads to a fuller realisation of what might be hidden within the plays. While this independent research may be unusual for a literary student, anyone who has worked on a theatre production will know that something of this sort remains to be done every time a Shakespeare play is prepared for performance: enactment always raises problems of realisation which no one seems to have met before. This is part of the continuing challenge of the texts and proves a spur to individual imagination.

Shakespeare's own life, at Stratford-upon-Avon and in London, as a member of a family, a landowner and a dramatist is of special interest to students of the plays. The main facts can be found in S. Schoenbaum's *William Shakespeare: A Compact Documentary Life* (1977), and there are several very readable accounts of his life in relation to his social background and theatre associations. The best of these are listed at the end of this volume and are readily available; but every reader has direct access to the most fascinating of all personal sources: the texts of the plays and poems read in chronological sequence of composition. Connections between play and play are made easily because words, phrases and actions are repeated and developed through Shakespeare's career.

Everyone can add to the speculations about why Shakespeare repeated this feature or that, and why he changed, omitted or added; and most students will enjoy doing so, even while remembering that none of these theories can ever be proved. The same is true of reflections of his personal life in the plays. About four years before writing *Hamlet*, Shakespeare had buried his only son, Hamnet, in the church at Stratford, but the effect of this on the relationships between fathers and sons which are so important in later history plays, *Hamlet* and *Lear*, lies far outside anyone's certain knowledge. The personal dimension of the plays' context raises a multitude of ideas that quicken our interest in the image of life inherent in the texts, and that is its most useful role: a source of speculation that gives rise to a very human engagement. It can be a further reach for our imagination.

☆

The ways in which a study of the original context of a play can serve an exploration of its theatrical life can better be exemplified than described. It may start with a reading of narrative and dramatic sources and then progress to other influential works, theatrical, literary and intellectual. It should include a survey of Shakespeare's other writings, both earlier and later. Nor should visual and domestic details be forgotten.

For an example I want to take Falstaff in *Henry IV, Parts One and Two*. He bestrides the two plays for which he was created so that he seems to take on a life of his own, transcending story, theme and argument, outstripping ordinary conceptions of what makes a good character for a play. He will frustrate our busy efforts to understand the meanings of every word he utters, or to relate his every action to some dramatic necessity or high artistic purpose. He has a life of his own that gives us little opportunity for purely objective study.

Proof of Falstaff's extraordinary life beyond the stage can be seen on all sides: in the large number of paintings and drawings that depict his various exploits, in uncountable imitations and in many eloquent disquisitions. A study of his character published in 1777 may be said to have started a whole school of Shakespearean criticism which is still active today. A large and exuberant autobiography of Falstaff by the poet, Robert Nye, has been published recently, and several operas with various Falstaffian titles are in the international repertoire. *The Shakespeare Allusion Book* – which is a good indication of immediate popular success and independent vitality – shows (in its revised edition of 1932) that in writings up to 1649 only Hamlet was mentioned more frequently than Falstaff; and that from 1650 to 1700 Falstaff reigned supreme, his 48 recorded allusions oustripping the mere 37 for Hamlet, his nearest rival. If allusions to Falstaff and to the two parts of *Henry IV* are added together, then these lead the field all the way, leaving *Hamlet*, prince and play, a poor second in both periods: 70 to 58 until the year 1649, and 79 to 37 thereafter.

The disarray of professional critics and scholars is more proof of Falstaff's vitality. He has left them divided, intellectually, morally and emotionally. One accuses another of being ill-informed, incomplete or insufficient; and also – more unusually – of being either unfeeling or soft-hearted. Article rebounds on article, and second thoughts often bring shifts of emphasis. Shakespeare seems to have foreseen this disagreement, making his hero boast how much there is to say 'in behalf of that Falstaff'. When we try to place Falstaff in his original context, we can start by compiling a brief genealogy.

He did not spring from Shakespeare's brain alone, but also from many books that he had read, plays he had seen, stories he had heard and real events he had experienced. His most obvious progenitor is Gluttony, who is evident in that 'fat beef', that 'huge bombard of sack, that stuff'd cloakbag of guts' (*Part One*: ii iv 435–6) and so on; or, to put the matter more flatteringly, as Falstaff would do when he was flying high, that 'plump Jack' (*Part One*: ii iv 462). This phrase of his own choosing is a reminder that Falstaff is also a 'Jack' and a 'staff' – although a staff that falls. The impotent and braggart lecher, who boasts in various plays and stories of his sexual conquests and chides everyone else for being promiscuous or unattractive, also contributed to the creation of Falstaff. So did the braggart soldier: bold and enterprising when all seems fair and his company is of the best, but 'roaring' and running away when the battle looks real and likely to be dangerous, or counterfeiting death, or sending others into the front line. All these predecessors of Falstaff can be found in earlier plays, especially morality plays, Roman comedies and French farces, and also in visual and verbal portrayals of the Seven Deadly Sins.

Alternative lineage can be traced in English religious and secular plays and folk entertainments. Falstaff is the 'Lord of Misrule', and the 'Vice' with dagger of lathe; he is 'Riot' and the 'Misleader' of youth. By no means least, he is also the 'Fool': at one vexed moment, 'Thou art a great Fool' (*Part Two*: II i 187) is the Lord Chief Justice's last word on the subject. In a later scene, the new king calls his old friend both 'fool and jester' (*Part Two*: v v 49), even as he commands Falstaff to abandon that ancient and special state of grace and, as any other old man, to 'fall to [his] prayers'. Falstaff can seem happy as the fool, playing with words, being mindful of his audience, imitating the puritans and making a virtue out of poverty, or at least a joke. But he is also the poor 'old man' close to death, who begs favour and money; he is the insinuating guest who will gull a friend to persuade him to be generous.

All these ancestors of Sir John Falstaff, Knight, can be identified explicitly in the words of Shakespeare's text, as if the author were proud of the forebears he had provided. But modern scholarship has not left the matter there. With *The Golden Bough* at one's elbow, Falstaff has been defined as the scapegoat who must be rejected to bring about the health and rebirth of the community: 'Falstaff', wrote J. I. M. Stewart, 'is in the end the dethroned and sacrificed king, the scapegoat.'[1] With Sigmund Freud's works to help, Falstaff has also been identified as a 'substitute father' whom Prince Hal has to kill, symbolically, before he can come of age and inherit his true father's real power. C. L. Barber opened up a still wider relevance, along the same lines of psychological and anthropological definition. He saw in Falstaff a Dionysiac power and influence. He called him the 'holiday pole of life', saying that his final rejection by Prince Hal, on the latter's becoming king, is Shakespeare's 'return to an official view of the sanctity of state'.[2] Professor Barber also argued that the dramatist achieved this resolution only by a 'sentimental use of magical relations', by a 'blurring of dramatic truths'. An alternative response would be to say that Falstaff, as 'Freedom' faced by his new king, is rather like the liberated, unpredictable, upstanding and entirely lovable Rosalind, who is faced at the end of *As You Like It* by Hymen, the God of Marriage. However, in that play the magic is evoked, if not stage-managed, by Freedom herself, whereas Professor Barber believed that neither Shakespeare nor Falstaff had any choice in the matter: the context controlled the drama, and so the play was botched and not concluded in good form.

Such an argument shows how wide a study of context may be and how relevant to an understanding of a play's theatrical life. But I have not yet enumerated all the energies from earlier dramatic works which met together in the creation of Falstaff. It is wonderful that such a distinctly individual person emerged, and with such limitless vitality. A scholar might agree with T. S. Eliot (himself one of the most culturally omnivorous poets of the present century) in chiding Shakespeare's generation of playwrights for 'their artistic greediness, their desire for every sort of effect together, their unwillingness to accept any limitation and abide by it'.[3]

An attempt to trace the origins of Falstaff will discover strong bonds with earlier persons in Shakespeare's own plays, especially those who are called upon to be actors or thrust themselves forward to perform. Like Bottom, Falstaff is ready for any role; like the earlier Worthies, in *Love's Labour's Lost*, he often does not know when the play is ended; like Julia in *The Two Gentlemen of Verona*, he can make his audience helpless with tears and, in his case, laughter. In Falstaff's scenes with Prince Hal, in both a mocking and a 'coming on disposition', I can catch traces also of Shakespeare's young lovers, who encounter each other with jests and word-play that draw truths to the surface of their thoughts which are out of the reach of either wisdom or downright folly.

The strange thing is – or it would be strange if bushes were never bears – that Falstaff seems to have derived from life itself, as well as the theatre. At first Shakespeare gave him another name, that of Sir John Oldcastle, and therefore must have intended him as a portrait of a real-life puritan hero from the family of the Lord Chamberlain who was the patron of the Chamberlain's Men, the acting company for which the plays of *Henry IV* were expressly written. Only a few traces – a joke or two and a reference in the Epilogue – remain as evidence of this phase of Falstaff's creation.

To divide Falstaff 'inventorially would dozy th'arithmetic of memory', and it is more convenient to sum up with the simple 'verity of extolment'. In creating him, Shakesphere drew upon the full range of his experience of theatre, life and books. So, while it is true that Falstaff stands alone, he can be understood more fully in the company of a large troop of forebears.

To whom can we compare Falstaff? Sir Toby Belch has been named as a minor relation, but he is so confined by the petty business on hand in *Twelfth Night*, so ready to depend on his niece and excuse himself by blaming the pickled herrings, that he leaves the play with only shreds of either dignity or wit. Besides, he has to contend with so much less than Falstaff: a mere ounce or two of 'malapert blood'. Bottom of *A Midsummer Night's Dream* has Falstaff's resilience and sense of adventure, but the greatest fancies of his mind are the gift of the Fairy Queen, and he dances out of his play in a clumsy Bergomask, at one with his fellows who have no inkling of his vision.

Rosalind, of *As You Like It*, is the more fit comparison. She can do 'strange things' (v ii 55), as well as see herself as a 'Barbary cock-pigeon' jealous over its hen, or 'more clamourous than a parrot against rain, more new-fangled than an ape, more giddy in her desires than a monkey'. She can 'weep for nothing, like Diana in the fountain', and will do that when her love is disposed to be merry (iv i 133–8). She knows that her thoughts 'run before her actions' and she cannot endure to be out of the sight of her Orlando. Rosalind may be nearest to Falstaff among all of Shakespeare's earlier creations, but she triumphs only in fancy, when she is almost alone in excitement and danger. Faced with unambiguous reality, she may faint or cry out in pain and hunger, like Irish wolves howling against the moon. Moreover, Shakespeare allowed her to resolve everything at the end of the play by the strategem of Hymen's appearance: anyone can be safe when a dramatist hatches such a miraculous plot. Falstaff was left to fend for himself, or pretend to do so; and he lives in a tough and sometimes very cruel world, not in the Forest of Arden.

For some strange reason, Shakespeare tried later to repeat the creation of Falstaff and failed outright. (Perhaps tradition is to be trusted here, and a royal decree over-ruled artistic commonsense and propriety.) For all the vigour of his dialogue and his physical bearing, the Falstaff of *The Merry Wives of Windsor* depends on the ladies for his small victories and on the age-old devices by which the action of the comedy is carried forward. *The Wives* is a good play with an almost magical ending, but its Falstaff and the journey he takes cannot be compared in achievement to those of *Henry IV, Parts One and Two*. Mistress Page sums up in right form:

> Good husband, let us every one go home,
> And laugh this sport o'er by a country fire;
> Sir John and all.

Shakespeare was not unjust to his newer creation, the second version of Falstaff, when he gave the last words of this comedy to the dynamic and much perplexed Master Ford.

To whom can we compare Sir John Falstaff in the plays of Shakespeare's contemporaries? Volpone, Sir Epicure Mammon and

Sir Giles Over-reach are penetrating, resourceful, and marvellously observed characters, but all of them are more narrowly conceived and draw more life from the mechanism of their comedies than from resources that seem to lie within their own beings. Thomas Dekker's Simon Eyre, in *The Shoemaker's Holiday*, is expansive and likable, but he was never put to any great test; he is at home only among his dependents and, for a brief subservient moment, with his king.

If we extend the search for Falstaff's equals into Shakespeare's later plays, the greatest tragedies provide the closest comparisons. I see the fat knight echoed in Hamlet, in the prince's wit and imagination, his sense of danger, make-believe and mockery, his affectionate responses to others and his ability to surprise – and in his author's inability to depict a world that allows his spirit to live in peace. When Fortinbras, succeeding to the Danish throne, tries to honour the dead, he cannot speak in due measure of Hamlet's greatness; nor can he stand in full possession of his inheritance.

But Hamlet, like Rosalind, is a young character who does not know the fardels, delays and failures of a long life. Parts of Falstaff's experience are mirrored only in the titanic figure of King Lear, especially in the scenes on the heath and on Dover beach, when he avoids justice, tries to wipe away mortality, hatches grotesque plans to recover his losses and, with unrepentant will, seeks to elude those who come to help him. At the end, like Falstaff, he finds only transitory peace, in a brief moment's thought that Cordelia might be alive. But this comparison is very limited too: Lear does not have Falstaff's comic resource and optimism; and, although he is changeable and wilful, he is far more isolated, inconsolable and dictatorial. Falstaff is a man who can live with folly and with poor, naked wretches. Moreover, he knows this when he is playing at being a monarch, the friend and cheat of all that he surveys.

What Hamlet, Lear and Falstaff share is Shakespeare's imagination working at full stretch, and his deep humanity. It is no wonder that the plays of *Henry IV, Parts One and Two* came to be known in Shakespeare's lifetime as *Falstaff, Parts One and Two*, or that they continued to be performed by the King's Men years after their author's death. And it is small wonder that *Part Two* was the less popular play, because the demands it makes upon actors and audience are as daunting as those plays of Shakespeare's that were seldom or never revived by the actors for whom they were written.

☆

So far I have considered Falstaff as if all he says and does is of equal importance. Good acting parts invite that kind of judgement: they have an inner unity, so that the actor does not stumble and falsify, or find the reality of his performance slipping away. But of Shakespeare's plays this is only a half-truth. One aspect and then others are shown to us in a sequence chosen by the dramatist, and it is very important to see how the changes occur during the progress of the action. Some elements drop away or return in other guises. Others appear as complete surprises well into the play: the depths of Falstaff's melancholy, for instance, are touched for the first time two Acts into the *Part Two*. But always the end of a play must pay for all, as the theatrical proverb reminds us. If Shakespeare failed to create a closer, truer or more affecting meeting of the audience with Falstaff in the last two Acts of *Part Two*, the role would be unworkable and no good actor would ever want to play it.

Good spirits start *Part One*: the interplay between Falstaff and Hal; the horse-play of the robbery; the old man's cry that 'They hate us youth!'; and the marvellous turning of the tables on Hal with 'By the lord, I knew ye as well as he that made ye', followed by the rousing self-portrait of Falstaff the lion, 'as valiant as Hercules', but by royal instinct unable to reveal all to a 'true prince'. Falstaff calls for blessings on everyone:

> . . . Gallants, lads, boys, hearts of gold, all the titles of good fellowship come to you! What, shall we be merry? Shall we have a play extempore?
> (*1*: II iv 268–71)

Now wider issues come into sharp focus: perhaps that is why, in nineteenth-century productions, the mock-play was cut for performance, as if too much might be given away. Falstaff pretends to be the King, using lofty terms, as heroic as they are sentimental; and he says much in praise of himself. Then Hal acts the King, his father, and demolishes Falstaff's boasts until he dares to challenge his self-knowledge. It is then that Falstaff, pretending to be Hal, acknowledges his old age and stakes his claim for attention:

> . . . No, my good lord: banish Peto, banish Bardolph, banish Poins; but for sweet Jack Falstaff, kind Jack Falstaff, true Jack Falstaff, valiant Jack Falstaff, and therefore more valiant being, as he is, old Jack Falstaff, banish not him thy Harry's company, banish not him thy Harry's company; banish plump Jack, and banish all the world.   (*1*: II iv 457–63)

Hal answers, 'I do, I will'. The climax of all the rhetoric, fantasy and affection, draws words from Hal that sound as if they do indeed come from the King his father – or from himself as he will be by the end of the plays. At that strangely real moment, the Sheriff is heard at the door with 'a monstrous watch', and every jest turns to absolute earnest. From now onwards, in both plays, Prince Hal is primarily a fighter for his realm and for his future, and Falstaff exists only on the borders of his life.

The same pattern can be seen in Shakespeare's handling of other strands of Falstaff's complex character. As an old man he will be outclassed by both Shallow and Silence, the old justices of Gloucestershire. As a braggart soldier he is totally eclipsed by the explosive and absurd Pistol – a difficult part to play because inner energy is required instantly at every entrance. On most of the later occasions when Falstaff is an actor, his audiences on-stage are far less attentive than formerly, especially Sir John Blount and the Lord Chief Justice. Shallow, Silence and other countrymen are so uncritical that they accept his performance as a Great Man of the Land with total belief, and so fail to supply the exciting edge of disbelief – or any really satisfying feed-lines. Falstaff is probably reeling drunk for his most extraordinary histrionic success, when that 'notable rebel', Sir John Colville of the Dale, capitulates without a stroke to Falstaff's mere reputation as a 'very Hercules'. Valiant Jack has no need here to counterfeit death, which was his way of escape in an earlier battle, and no need for Prince John to connive in his story, in order to claim heroic stature. Falstaff is briefly Fortune's minion; but his victory is unearned and so it gives him proportionally less satisfaction.

Falstaff's roles as the Vice or Riot, or the Misleader of youth – with which Hal as King taxes him at the very end – are almost non-existent in *Part Two*, for the simple reason that Prince Hal is no longer around. Prince John would not listen to his views on Sherrysack and so the theatre audience is given them direct, in soliloquy. The Prince and Poins do disguise themselves as drawers in *Part Two* (Act II, scene iv) to get a rise out of Falstaff, but on this occasion the game falls flat as soon as they unmask. And before then we know that Hal's deepest thoughts are now elsewhere:

> . . . my heart bleeds inwardly that my father is so sick; . . .
>
> . . . thus we play the fools with the time, and the spirits of the wise sit in the clouds and mock us.   (*2*: II ii 45–6; 135–6)

But much that is new is revealed about Falstaff in *Part Two*. We see him in prosperity, attended by a page, thinking absurdly of a new-found dignity, new clothes and prayers. We see him with the Hostess, imposing on 'the easy-yielding spirit of this woman' (*2*: II i 110–11) and on her stupidity. We see him affectionate and gentle with Doll Tearsheet, knowing how to save 'the sweetest morsel of the night' when every one else is conspiring to leave it 'unpicked' (lines 354–5). Doll is both ludicrous and cunning; she knows when to call her suitor a 'fat fool' and when to come running all 'blubber'd' at his bidding. Poins's phrase 'dead elm' is not fit for Falstaff in this scene, for here his life seems to become easy and even sufficient.

Despite his conquest of Colville (III ii), Falstaff's return to the wars has already shown him to be prepared for any mean stratagem that will save his own exertion and refill his purse. He sends only the most willing or the most helpless off to battle. The amusement he gains at the expense of old acquaintances, now country justices, is undemanding fun, so that he turns progressively towards the audience when he expresses his own purposes and wit. Tactfully, Shakespeare has Falstaff off-stage when Master Feeble shows that a simple mind need not be 'base':

> . . . No man's too good to serve's Prince. And let it go which way it will, he that dies this year is quit for the next. (*2*: III ii 231–2)

At the end of the recruiting episode in this scene, Falstaff has little but reminiscence to share with the audience, and perhaps some new self-knowledge: 'Lord, lord, how subject we old men are to this vice of lying!' (lines 294–5).

Some critics have argued that Shakespeare was losing his grip at this point, or becoming dissatisfied with the wiles of his old favourite. But I think quite the reverse: the play is moving on to another part of the forest of Shakespeare's creative mind. The first Gloucestershire episode ends with Falstaff promising to return and fleece these two old friends of some of their comforts and their money: a promise repeated immediately after Prince John's inglorious victory. Shakespeare is setting things up for the greatest of Falstaff's apotheoses. He has given him comparatively little to say in the two scenes of the return to Gloucestershire, but Falstaff sails into this haven, establishing himself without effort in a world of ease and good fellowship.

Before the battles of *Part One* Shakespeare had introduced a scene, with music in the air, in which the warriors had lain down on the 'wanton rushes' to hear a young bride sing in mysterious Welsh to her young husband (*1*: III i 213). It is a season of calm and peace, more effective in performance than any reading of the play could suggest. It is an amazing contrast to the jars of rebellion and suspicion, and is presided over by the fatherly Glendower who seems able to conjure musicians from the vasty deeps to harmonise this brief domestic idyll. The episode has no companion in the second half of *Part One*, and the audience has to wait until Act v of *Part Two* before catching a full echo of its power. Falstaff is no great warrior, nor are his cronies strict justices; but their reappearance together in Act v, scenes i and iii, is handled with supreme delicacy and tact. The effect is calm and miraculous: a seemingly impossible transformation.

Realistic details are provided about a couple of short-legged hens,

William the Cook and the 'sack he lost the other day at Hinckley Fair', about the sowing of 'the headland' with red wheat, about a 'new link' for an old bucket, and much more – all quite unusual, not only in Shakespeare's plays but also in any others of the period. These rural and domestic details set the scene in our imagination. Falstaff blusters to the audience at first, speaking like a trickster in a play by Jonson who is about to feed fat upon his gulls. But when Shallow entices him ('You shall see my orchard, where in an arbor, we will eat a last year's pippin of mine own graffing, with a dish of caraways, and so forth . . . And then to bed'), Falstaff is seemingly bewitched, so that his melancholy and self-interest evaporate.

His appreciation sounds unaffected: "Fore God, you have here a goodly dwelling and rich' (2: v iii 4). He might still be thinking of his own pickings to come, but he uses the words of the *Book of Deuteronomy* in the Bishop's Bible version, where it speaks of the promised land for God's chosen people:

Yea, and when thou hast eaten and filled thyself, and hast built goodly houses, and dwelt therein:
And when thy beasts and thy sheep are waxen many, and thy silver and gold is multiplied, and all that thou hast is increased:
Then beware lest thine heart rise, and thou forget the Lord thy God which brought thee out of the land of Egypt, and from the house of bondage:
. . . for to humble thee, and to prove thee, and that he might do thee good at the latter end.   (*Deut.*, viii 12–14, 16)

Falstaff 'at the latter end' of the play enjoys 'a goodly dwelling and rich' without a struggle for dominance in wit, deceit or good spirits. When Master Silence breaks into song, Falstaff at once claims kinship with his 'merry heart'. The songs celebrate good fellowship – and one is appropriate to pre-Lenten relaxation, the end of a long winter, when ' 'Tis merry in hall when beards wag all'. Several other references in the text indicate that Shakespeare has imagined all this happening on an unexpectedly balmy afternoon in early spring: the white wheat that stands through winter has been sown already, and the headlands are due to be sown with the red (or spring) wheat; they have supped on mutton because the year's new lambs are not yet fattened; some pippins remain from last year's harvest. As Silence expands marvellously in confidence, his songs hang in the air like Feste's at the end of *Twelfth Night*. But they are different in their dramatic purpose: Silence is now a man of 'mettle' and, as Shallow proudly asserts, any one of them may 'speak as a king' and 'lack nothing' of any consequence.

This old men's carnival, as a new year break into life, slows down the whole narrative of the play and causes the audience to forget the great business of politics and government. In practical theatre-terms, the business of the scene cannot be rushed, because there are many complicated actions that have to be carried out carefully and variously. And the audience, too, must be quiet if they are to catch the weak voice of Silence before he is taken gently off to bed. Like the musical scene in *Part One*, this country idyll makes comparatively little effect in reading, but in performance is it as wonderful and 'strange' as the concluding scenes of the *Merchant*, *As You Like It*, the *Dream* or *Twelfth Night*.

Perhaps its inspiration came from a fine afternoon early in 1598 – the dates are absolutely right – when, after a long winter, Shakespeare sat in his new garden and thought about future retirement to his old father's countryside. This would have been in the so-called 'Great Garden' of New Place which he had bought in 1597; this garden, complete with an orchard and attached to the second largest house in the country town of Stratford, had been enlarged to an unusual size by an earlier owner's purchase of land belonging to the Priory of Pinley.

The scene's effect on an audience can be great. Falstaff no longer pushes for attention, he is at ease; he floats through the scene a model of courtesy, generous, open and of a free disposition, forgetful of all else. We follow him in imagination. Many of Shakespeare's greatest roles close with little to say at the very end – Rosalind, King Lear and, comparatively speaking, Hamlet: the audience has possessed them fully and in imagination lives, or dies, with them.

Although these contented moments in a country garden grow in our imaginations and outreach verbal analysis, Shakespeare had a further journey for Falstaff to take in this play. Pistol arrives late at that glorious party with the news of the death of Henry the Fourth, and Falstaff is off at once to London. He rides through the night towards a confrontation from which he expects a renewal of life and hopes.

In due time Hal arrives in full procession, as King Henry the Fifth, and Falstaff cries aloud (*2*: v v 41): 'God save thy Grace, King Hal, my royal Hal!' This is a splendid prayer and greeting; or a splendid performance. But the King does not answer, and Falstaff is drawn on: 'God save thee, my sweet boy!' Still no answer comes, but the King has a curt word with the Lord Chief Justice because Falstaff has now become an old man making a nuisance of himself. The dignified official questions the sanity of the affectionate and unruly greetings:

Have you your wits? Know you what 'tis you speak?

To this Falstaff's reply is very simple and very grand:

My king! My Jove! I speak to thee, my heart!

It is then that Hal speaks:

> I know thee not, old man. Fall to thy prayers.
> How ill white hairs become a fool and jester. . . .

The contrast is one of the greatest in Shakespeare's plays, brilliantly prepared for, as much by Hal's growing prudence and closeness to the seat of power as by Falstaff's melancholy, his tenderness and impudence to Doll Tearsheet, and then his unexpected warmth and ease in Gloucestershire; and also by Feeble's brave resolve to serve his prince and risk his life. Henry the Fifth prolongs the agony of encounter, in words that show far more tension and inner pressures than those of his earlier confident soliloquy: 'I know you all and will awhile uphold/The unyok'd humour of your idleness . . .' (*1*: 1 ii 188ff.). There is no easy rhetorical climax, no self-contented egotism:

> I have long dreamt of such a kind of man,
> So surfeit-swell'd, so old, and so profane,
> But, being awak'd, I do despise my dream.
> Make less thy body hence, and more thy grace; . . .

And so on to a public declaration of his necessary transformation into monarch. He acknowledges former folly and promises future wisdom. He banishes this misleader of his youth who 'on pain of death' may come no nearer to his person than ten miles. Hal plays safe and cold, and probably sweats as he does so. Falstaff does not reply; only when the King has gone does he turn to his new-found old friend: 'Master Shallow, I owe you a thousand pounds.' As his courage slowly rallies, he pronounces that he will be 'sent for soon at night'. But then the Chief Justice reappears and orders him to detention in the Fleet prison. Falstaff expostulates for a moment, but has no coherent reply. Braggart Pistol has the last word as the small party is led away: '*Si fortuna me tormenta, spero me contenta.*'

What exactly is Hal banishing from his public life? Falstaff has no power, no reasonable wisdom, no constancy or trustworthiness, little courage; even his vitality is failing. He is a man whom we have seen to be cowardly, immoral, deceitful, greedy, irresponsible. He is a fool, a jester, a profane and surfeit-swollen 'misleader' of a prince, as the text makes plain at this very moment. But he is also a man capable of three sovereign virtues. First of all, he is imaginative; his mind creates great and surprising dreams, and these send his thoughts and words, and sometimes himself, towards marvellous exploits and great content.

Secondly, he is a man who is nearly always restless and unappeased; until overcome with weariness or until he is able to welcome an unlooked for and settled peace, he is always reaching out towards new adventure. And thirdly, he is a man capable of good fellowship, of speaking to the hearts of men and women.

It is at this point that a study of the context of Shakespeare's play leads back to speculative and imaginative engagement in the drama. The nature of the play's theatrical life leads me to think that Shakespeare arranged for Hal to banish Falstaff so dramatically because the dramatist was exploring what it would be like to banish those human qualities with which he could most readily associate his own hopes. That may be why Falstaff lives with such vitality today.

There are critics who believe that we should side, gladly, with Henry against Falstaff, and that only romantic irresponsibility could think otherwise. They quote Elizabethan politicians and moralists to prove their point. But other scholars argue that the ending is muffed and dramatic tensions are unresolved. A few take Hal as the portrait of a self-seeking and cunning man of power, and find cruelty and inhumanity in his last speech. The text provides evidence for all these contrary judgements, and Elizabethan writers and social beliefs can support each one. But I would argue that the fascination which Falstaff exerts over us and the excitement of the banishment can be explained only if Shakespeare gave to Falstaff enduring values that were at least as close to his own heart as those of the responsible head of state.

Renaissance minds were not always so sober or single-minded as are those of critics who try to interpret the plays of Shakespeare. Towards the end of *The Praise of Folly*, Erasmus makes Folly quote from *Ecclesiastes*, vii 4: 'The heart of the wise is the home of sadness and the heart of the foolish is the home of joy.' The contented folly of the scenes in Gloucestershire implies much the same message, and Shallow is present at the close of the play to remind us of that happiness. Narrow conventions of art, thought and life are left behind: Falstaff outstrips all comparisons and lives in the imagination of countless audiences.

☆

No one today would assume that an imaginative author speaks directly to us in his own person in his writings. We are very aware of the conscious and unconscious subterfuges which disguise personal commitment. But there are exceptions, as confessed by Somerset Maugham who was a constant disguiser of himself:

The writer of fiction can only adequately create characters that are aspects of himself. Others he describes, he does not create, and they seldom carry conviction. And if this is true it follows that by studying the characters with which an author has best succeeded, which he has presented with most sympathy and understanding, you should be able to get a more complete idea of his nature than any biography can give you.[4]

If Maugham has recognised a truth, a study of the context of Shakespeare's plays should always be accompanied by a lively experience of their life in performance and in the imaginations of readers and audiences: we must notice where the plays most fully and deeply 'carry conviction'. This will lead us beyond literary concepts of character, action or theme, and may bring us closer to understanding the dramatist himself.

13 | *Engagement*

... I have considered, our whole life is like a *Play*: wherein everyman, forgetful of himself, is in travail with expression of another.   ...[1]

Ben Jonson's words touch on a sense of theatre that is implicit in Shakespeare's plays. Our involvement with the plays is both intimate and strange; we lose ordinary bearings and find ourselves drawn into unfamiliar worlds where 'everything seems double'.[2]

At first we may be lost, but the persons of the drama become more open to us as we are drawn forward by the developing action and as they respond to forces that seem hidden within themselves. The actors give more and more to the parts they play; and, when all is finished, the actors, their parts and their audience are all more clearly themselves and all closer together. This process is neither easy nor direct, and we will soon understand that, if the author knew where all the words and actions would lead as he wrote the early scenes, he has concealed that knowledge very thoroughly. But the effect is assured: no matter what emotions, thoughts and deeds have been produced during the course of the performance, the conclusion brings heightened pleasure, awareness and unity; then the play is most itself, and most able to reflect and define the very beings of those who, in their different ways, re-create it. A large measure of self-forgetfulness is a necessary ingredient in this happening, so that everyone may make a true discovery of what the author can evoke from them.

What happens in a theatre can also happen in the minds of readers and students. To achieve this, they must be open, free, honest and personal when they engage with a text; and they must respond as both actors and audience respond, so that the play can have its double life and its continuous sense of exploration. These are primary responsibilities, and failure to accept them reduces any play to verbal debate, elaborate poem, gallery of characters or slow-moving narrative. Students who start by trying to define meanings will grasp only a part of the drama, while the heart of the matter escapes every well-wrought net of theory or philosophy. Critical questions *are* important, of course, and Shakespeare's text will suggest many answers, in the same way as they offer many poetic, iconographic and literary pleasures; but critical questions should follow, and not precede, an imaginative, personal and adventurous process of discovery that is similar to an actor's engagement in rehearsal and performance. That is why I started this 'new guide' to the plays by showing how an actor brings life to his part, and how both reader and student can respond to Shakespeare's texts as the actor does.

For some years it has been a critical commonplace that Shakespeare saw his characters as actors and the world as a stage. Describing his appearance and behaviour, Hamlet declares that these are 'actions that a man might play' (i ii 84). Coriolanus knows that

> You have put me now to such a part which never
> I shall discharge to th' life.   (*Cor.*, iii ii 105–6)

Troilus finishes by choosing one performance in preference to another:

> . . .   With comfort go;
> Hope of revenge shall hide our inward woe.   (*T. & C.*, v x 30–1)

Richard the Second revalues his earlier performance and his audience's responses:

> For you have but mistook me all this while.
> I live with bread like you, feel want,
> Taste grief, need friends: subjected thus,
> How can you say to me I am a king?   (*R.II*, iii ii 174–7)

At the very beginning of *Othello*, Iago teases Roderigo with his power to hide deepest feelings: 'I am not what I am' (i i 66); and later the Moor experiences the pain of pretence – 'O hardness to dissemble!' (iii iv 31) – when he has lost belief in Desdemona's goodness. So thoroughly did the idea of men and women as actors enter Shakespeare's consciousness that the texts allude on many occasions to performance, disguise and truth-to-life without the terminology of the theatre. On the other hand, the notion of the stage can take over from ordinary talk; Macbeth sums up the whole of life in its terms:

> Life's but a walking shadow, a poor player,
> That struts and frets his hour upon the stage,
> And then is heard no more;   . . .   (*Mac.*, v v 24–6)

In *As You Like It*, Jaques proclaims more expansively that 'All the world's a stage' (ii viii 139); and on Dover Beach, near the end of his greatest misery, Lear counsels patience on 'this great stage of fools' (*Lear*, iv vi 184).

But recognition should not stop here. Shakespeare's thoughts *were* quickened by the idea of actors and a stage but, more than this, his consciousness was fully involved with actors in performance. No element of an actor's experience was unknown to him or without its fascination. He imagined complete human beings in action; he sensed their physical, instinctive, technical and personal performances, their interactions, their collaborative search for truth and fulfilment. To realise his plays in our imagination, we have to think and feel as actors, and as audiences in immediate relationship to those actors. Imaginatively we should become at one with what happens in the play, and give all we can to that experience.

This lively engagement will not provide ready answers for the old critical questions: sometimes it will make them appear irrelevant, unhelpful, or impossibly difficult. But when those questions are posed once more – What is Shakespearean tragedy? What was Shakespeare's view of history, politics and society? Can you explain the attraction of the comedies? – answers will come, more slowly than before, but with an assurance that can be bred only of experience. We will report and judge as travellers do, and not as geographers who have stayed at home, studied maps, theorised, and listened to others.

Suggestions for
Further Reading

This booklist gives references for all the books to which the reader has been directed in the text as providing sources for further enquiry and study. Other works also are included, with notes of their relevance.

ACTING (chapter 5)

Christine Edwards, *The Stanislavski Heritage* (New York, 1965; London, 1966). A useful companion to Stanislavski's writings (see below).
Rudolf Laban, *The Mastery of Movement,* revised by Lisa Ullman (London, 1960 and subsequent reprintings). The revised edition incorporates improvements planned by Laban, as well as some rewriting and additions by Lisa Ullman.
Robert Lewis, *Method–or Madness?* (New York, 1958; London, 1960). A popular and practical account of Stanislavskian acting.
Sonia Moore, *The Stanislavsky System* (2nd edn, New York, 1965; London, 1966). This contains simple exercises in a graded sequence whereby a practical awareness may be gained of Stanislavski's teaching.
Constantin Stanislavski:
  My Life in Art (New York and London, 1924; paperback, London, 1979);
  An Actor Prepares (New York, 1936; London, 1937; paperback, London, 1979);
  Building a Character (New York, 1949; London, 1950; paperback, London, 1979);
  Creating a Role (New York, 1961; London, 1963; paperback, London, 1981).

SHAKESPEARE'S TEXT (chapter 7)

A New English Dictionary on Historical Principles, edited by James A. H. Murray, Henry Bradley *et al.* (Oxford, 1888–1933).
John Bartlett, *A Complete Concordance to the Works of Shakespeare* (London, 1894; new impression, London, 1953).

E. A. Abbott, *A Shakespearian Grammar* (3rd edn, London, 1872). Still very serviceable, especially as a means of finding parallel usages in Shakespeare's works.

E. J. Dobson, *English Pronunciation. 1500–1700* (2nd edn, Oxford, 1968).

Sir Walter W. Greg, *The Shakespeare First Folio: Its Bibliographical and Textual History* (Oxford, 1955, and subsequent reprints).

Sister Miriam Joseph, *Shakespeare's Use of the Arts of Language* (New York, 1947). A shortened version of this is available in paperback: *Rhetoric in Shakespeare's Time* (New York and London, 1962).

C. T. Onions, *A Shakespeare Glossary* (final revision, Oxford, 1953; now available in paperback).

L. A. Sonnino, *A Handbook to Sixteenth-Century Rhetoric* (London, 1968).

STAGING (chapter 11)

Sally Beauman, *The Royal Shakespeare Company's Centenary Production of 'Henry V'* (Oxford, 1976).

Peter Brook, *The Empty Space* (London, 1968; paperback edition, 1972).

John Russell Brown, *Free Shakespeare* (London, 1974; available in paperback).

Rosamond Gilder, *John Gielgud's Hamlet* (New York and London, 1937).

Harley Granville-Barker, *Prefaces to Shakespeare*, series of 6 volumes (London, 1927–47; now available in paperback). Gives accounts of how specific plays could be staged.

Grigori Kozintsev, *King Lear: The Space of Tragedy* (1977). This diary of a film director is informed by his work in the theatre.

STAGE HISTORIES (chapter 11)

The following are among the growing number of studies of Shakespeare's plays in performance from his own day to our own:

Dennis Bartholomeusz, *Macbeth and the Players* (Cambridge, 1969)

Marvin Rosenberg, *The Masks of Othello* (Berkeley, Cal. and London, 1961).

A. C. Sprague, *Shakespeare's Histories: Plays for the Stage* (London, 1964).

CONTEXT (chapter 12)

A New Companion to Shakespeare Studies, edited by Kenneth Muir and S. Schoenbaum (Cambridge, 1971; available in paperback).

Select Bibliographical Guides: Shakespeare, edited by Stanley Wells (Oxford, 1973; available in paperback).

Shakespeare Quarterly (Folger Shakespeare Library, Washington DC) and *Shakespeare Survey* (Cambridge) publish every year bibliographies of new contributions to Shakespeare studies.

Muriel Bradbrook, *The Growth and Structure of Elizabethan Comedy* (London, 1955).

Geoffrey Bullough, *Narrative and Dramatic Sources of Shakespeare*, 8 volumes (London, 1958–75).

Wolfgang Clemen, *English Tragedy Before Shakespeare: The Development of Dramatic Speech*: English translation (London, 1961) of German original (Munich, 1955).

Madeleine Doran, *Endeavors of Art: A Study of Form in Elizabethan Drama* (Madison, Wisc. and London, 1954; available in paperback).

Irving Ribner, *The English History Play in the Age of Shakespeare* (Princeton, N.J., 1957).

A. P. Rossiter, *English Drama from Early Times to the Elizabethans* (London, 1950). A short and eminently readable introduction, which surveys classical and folk sources as well as the plays of Shakespeare's predecessors.

Leo Salingar, *Shakespeare and the Tradition of Comedy* (Cambridge, 1974; available in paperback).

F. P. Wilson, *The English Drama, 1485–1585* (Oxford, 1969).

Peter Laslett, *The World We Have Lost* (London, 1965; 2nd edn, 1971, available in paperback).

Lawrence Stone:
> *The Crisis of the Aristocracy, 1558–1641* (Oxford, 1965; available in paperback); *The Family, Sex and Marriage in England, 1500–1800* (New York and London, 1977; abridged, paperback edition, 1979).

Shakespeare's England: An Account of the Life and Manners of His Age, edited by Sir Sidney Lee and C. T. Onions, 2 vols (Oxford, 1916 and subsequent reprintings).

Shakespeare in His Own Age, edited by Allardyce Nicoll (first published in 1964 as a special issue of *Shakespeare Survey*, XVII; new edn, Cambridge, 1976, available in paperback).

Muriel Bradbrook, *Shakespeare: The Poet in His World* (London, 1978).

Sir Edmund K. Chambers, *Shakespeare: A Study of Facts and Problems* (Oxford, 1930).

S. Schoenbaum, *William Shakespeare: A Compact Documentary Life* (New York, 1977: an abridgement of Schoenbaum's major work (New York and London, 1975).

Index

For references to Shakespeare's plays, see under Shakespeare.

Notes

2   SHAKESPEARE DEAD AND ALIVE

1. *The Guardian*, 3 August 1977.

3   CONTEMPORARY SHAKESPEARE

1. *Timber*, in C. H. Herford and P. and E. Simpson (eds), *Works of Ben Jonson*, 11 vols (Oxford, 1925–52): vol. VIII, p. 637.
2. Ibid., vol. I, pp. 151, 141.
3. Edward Bond, Introduction, *Plays: Two* (London, 1978), p. *ix*.
4. Ibid., p. *ix*.
5. *A Midsummer Night's Dream*: v i 66.
6. Ibid., IV i 203–4.

4   PARTS FOR ACTORS

1. Quoted in Sir Edmund K. Chambers, *The Elizabethan Stage* (Oxford, 1923), vol. IV, pp. 369–70.
2. Thomas Heywood, *An Apology for Actors* (1612), p. 20.
3. *Pierce Penniless, his Supplication to the Devil*, ed. Stanley Wells (Stratford-upon-Avon Library, 1964), p. 65.
4. Fynes Moryson, *Shakespeare's Europe*, ed. C. Hughes (London, 1903), p. 304.

5   PLAYS FOR ACTORS

1. *The Times*, 31 December 1979.

7   SHAKESPEARE'S TEXT

1. *Timber*, in *Works*, op. cit., vol. VIII, p. 584.

2. Sigurd Burckhardt, *Shakespearean Meanings* (Princeton, N.J., 1968)
3. See J. Russell Brown, 'The Compositors of *Hamlet* Q2 and *The Mer Venice*', *Studies in Bibliography*, VII (1955), pp. 39–40.

8   SPEECH

1. *Works of John Keats*, edited by H. Buxton Forman (Glasgow, 1901) p. 230.

9   MOTIVATION AND SUBTEXT

1. Even the following 'board' may have a sexual tone, in that 'bed an was what the husband promised to his wife in the wedding ceremor English marriage rite: Hymen uses the phrase at the conclusion of *As y* (v iv 136).
2. See Beatrice's use of 'intermingle' in *Much Ado* (v ii 55).
3. See, for example, similar usages in *Othello*: Roderigo's 'solicitati 199), and Iago's talk of Cassio's 'soliciting' (II iii 375).

10   SHOWS FOR AUDIENCES

1. Interview with Kenneth Harris, *Observer*, 2 February 1969.

11   STAGE ACTION

1. Hamlet: I ii 85; I iv 39; I v 189–90; III i 63–4; III ii 380; III iv 212; IV iv 43–4; v i 263; v ii 67–8; v ii 230–1; v ii 330.
2. F. W. Nietzsche, *The Birth of Tragedy* (1872): English tran F. Golffing (New York, 1956) pp. 141, 144 and 103.
3. See *The Winter's Tale*: IV iv 87–97.

12   CONTEXT

1. J. I. M. Stewart, *Character and Motive in Shakespeare* (London, 19
2. C. L. Barber, *Shakespeare's Festive Comedy* (Princeton, N.J., 195
3. T. S. Eliot, *Elizabethan Essays* (London, 1934), p. 18.
4. Somerset Maugham, *A Writer's Notebook* (London, 1969), p.

13   ENGAGEMENT

1. *Timber*, in *Works*, op. cit., vol. VIII, p. 597.
2. *A Midsummer Night's Dream*: IV i 187.

Muriel Bradbrook, *The Growth and Structure of Elizabethan Comedy* (London, 1955).

Geoffrey Bullough, *Narrative and Dramatic Sources of Shakespeare*, 8 volumes (London, 1958–75).

Wolfgang Clemen, *English Tragedy Before Shakespeare: The Development of Dramatic Speech*: English translation (London, 1961) of German original (Munich, 1955).

Madeleine Doran, *Endeavors of Art: A Study of Form in Elizabethan Drama* (Madison, Wisc. and London, 1954; available in paperback).

Irving Ribner, *The English History Play in the Age of Shakespeare* (Princeton, N.J., 1957).

A. P. Rossiter, *English Drama from Early Times to the Elizabethans* (London, 1950). A short and eminently readable introduction, which surveys classical and folk sources as well as the plays of Shakespeare's predecessors.

Leo Salingar, *Shakespeare and the Tradition of Comedy* (Cambridge, 1974; available in paperback).

F. P. Wilson, *The English Drama, 1485–1585* (Oxford, 1969).

Peter Laslett, *The World We Have Lost* (London, 1965; 2nd edn, 1971, available in paperback).

Lawrence Stone:
The Crisis of the Aristocracy, 1558–1641 (Oxford, 1965; available in paperback); *The Family, Sex and Marriage in England, 1500–1800* (New York and London, 1977; abridged, paperback edition, 1979).

Shakespeare's England: An Account of the Life and Manners of His Age, edited by Sir Sidney Lee and C. T. Onions, 2 vols (Oxford, 1916 and subsequent reprintings).

Shakespeare in His Own Age, edited by Allardyce Nicoll (first published in 1964 as a special issue of *Shakespeare Survey*, XVII; new edn, Cambridge, 1976, available in paperback).

Muriel Bradbrook, *Shakespeare: The Poet in His World* (London, 1978).

Sir Edmund K. Chambers, *Shakespeare: A Study of Facts and Problems* (Oxford, 1930).

S. Schoenbaum, *William Shakespeare: A Compact Documentary Life* (New York, 1977: an abridgement of Schoenbaum's major work (New York and London, 1975).

Notes

2 SHAKESPEARE DEAD AND ALIVE

1. *The Guardian*, 3 August 1977.

3 CONTEMPORARY SHAKESPEARE

1. *Timber*, in C. H. Herford and P. and E. Simpson (eds), *Works of Ben Jonson*, 11 vols (Oxford, 1925–52): vol. VIII, p. 637.
2. Ibid., vol. I, pp. 151, 141.
3. Edward Bond, Introduction, *Plays: Two* (London, 1978), p. *ix*.
4. Ibid., p. *ix*.
5. *A Midsummer Night's Dream*: v i 66.
6. Ibid., IV i 203–4.

4 PARTS FOR ACTORS

1. Quoted in Sir Edmund K. Chambers, *The Elizabethan Stage* (Oxford, 1923), vol. IV, pp. 369–70.
2. Thomas Heywood, *An Apology for Actors* (1612), p. 20.
3. *Pierce Penniless, his Supplication to the Devil*, ed. Stanley Wells (Stratford-upon-Avon Library, 1964), p. 65.
4. Fynes Moryson, *Shakespeare's Europe*, ed. C. Hughes (London, 1903), p. 304.

5 PLAYS FOR ACTORS

1. *The Times*, 31 December 1979.

7 SHAKESPEARE'S TEXT

1. *Timber*, in *Works*, op. cit., vol. VIII, p. 584.

2. Sigurd Burckhardt, *Shakespearean Meanings* (Princeton, N.J., 1968), p. *vii*.

3. See J. Russell Brown, 'The Compositors of *Hamlet* Q2 and *The Merchant of Venice*', *Studies in Bibliography*, VII (1955), pp. 39–40.

8 SPEECH

1. *Works of John Keats*, edited by H. Buxton Forman (Glasgow, 1901), vol. v, p. 230.

9 MOTIVATION AND SUBTEXT

1. Even the following 'board' may have a sexual tone, in that 'bed and board' was what the husband promised to his wife in the wedding ceremony of the English marriage rite: Hymen uses the phrase at the conclusion of *As you Like It* (v iv 136).

2. See Beatrice's use of 'intermingle' in *Much Ado* (v ii 55).

3. See, for example, similar usages in *Othello*: Roderigo's 'solicitation' (IV ii 199), and Iago's talk of Cassio's 'soliciting' (II iii 375).

10 SHOWS FOR AUDIENCES

1. Interview with Kenneth Harris, *Observer*, 2 February 1969.

11 STAGE ACTION

1. Hamlet: I ii 85; I iv 39; I v 189–90; III i 63–4; III ii 380; III iv 212; IV iii 51–2; IV iv 43–4; v i 263; v ii 67–8; v ii 230–1; v ii 330.

2. F. W. Nietzsche, *The Birth of Tragedy* (1872): English translation by F. Golffing (New York, 1956) pp. 141, 144 and 103.

3. See *The Winter's Tale*: IV iv 87–97.

12 CONTEXT

1. J. I. M. Stewart, *Character and Motive in Shakespeare* (London, 1949), p. 139.

2. C. L. Barber, *Shakespeare's Festive Comedy* (Princeton, N.J., 1959), p. 220.

3. T. S. Eliot, *Elizabethan Essays* (London, 1934), p. 18.

4. Somerset Maugham, *A Writer's Notebook* (London, 1969), p. 334.

13 ENGAGEMENT

1. *Timber*, in *Works*, op. cit., vol. VIII, p. 597.

2. *A Midsummer Night's Dream*: IV i 187.

Index

For references to Shakespeare's plays, see under Shakespeare.